Crochet Donut Buddies

Rachel Zain

DAVID & CHARLES

www.davidandcharles.com

Contents

Dedication

This book is dedicated to my Grandmother, Joan, who taught me how to crochet many years ago and to my Grandmother, Sally, for always believing in me and supporting me. To my mother, Karen and father John, who have always pushed me to do better even when times were tough and finally to my children - you are my inspiration and the reason I pick up my hook every day.

Welcome

Hi! Welcome to my Donut Buddy Crochet Book. My name is Rachel, and I'm so excited for you to be here with me! I am a British crochet pattern designer born in England.

My love of crochet started when I was just eight years old. I used to watch my grandmother knitting and crocheting in her favourite chair, which I found fascinating - how someone could simply take a "stick" and yarn and create such beautiful things was beyond me! It wasn't until she saw me watching with such interest when she gifted me my own hook and some yarn that I truly fell in love with it. I still have that hook 25 years later, as it reminds me of where my crochet journey started.

Fast forward 15 years from when I first picked up that hook to when my crochet journey really began. I had just given birth to my first son, and I really wanted to make him some Amigurumi toys, just as my nan had made for me when I was small - this is where my love of Amigurumi came from. So I picked up my hook and yarn and created my first Amigurumi bunny. I fell in love all over again. I decided Amigurumi was for me, so in 2019 I opened my Instagram page and Etsy store **Oodles of Crochet**, and when my second son was born, I designed Donut Buddies! Fun, cute, kawaii character donuts designed specifically for smaller babies and children.

Many crochet artists have made them - mothers, fathers, grandparents and more, both beginner and advanced, for their families and loved ones.

There are 50 Donut Buddy patterns to dive into, each with their very own skill level, so it doesn't matter if you are a beginner 'Amigurumist' or an advanced crocheter; there is something for everyone to try. The great thing is you can mix and match colours and styles to create your own unique variations!

Donut Buddies are perfect for imaginative play with your baby. Head off on a secret safari around the home, play Donut Buddy tea party, and group the animals into sets or colours for a great learning experience!

You can use a smaller hook and yarn weight to create baby-friendly holiday decorations and nursery decor or use a larger hook and yarn weight for snuggly plush child-friendly home decor. This book is my way of spreading the joy and happiness of my Donut Buddy Amigurumi work; I always say that the best part about these Donuts is that they are calorie-free!

So have fun creating these cute buddies. I have a feeling you're going to love them as much as I do.

Happy crocheting,

Rachel Zain

HOW TO USE THIS BOOK

Skill level

Every pattern in my book is marked with a little Donut skill level to indicate how easy they are to make. From one Donut, designed for beginners, up to five Donuts for intermediate and advanced crocheters.

Working in the round

The Basic Donuts are worked in the round (see **Crochet Techniques**) as a continuous spiral. Some of the accessories are worked in rows.

How to read a pattern

It's a good idea to read through the full pattern you wish to use before making a start so that you are familiar with the steps. Each line of the pattern refers to a Round or Row as marked at the beginning.

Use a stitch marker to mark the last stitch of the previous round and then follow the pattern for the next round, which will take you back to the stitch marker. Reposition the marker for the next round.

Abbreviations are used throughout this book. Refer back to the Abbreviations list (see **Basic Donut Pattern**) if you are not sure what they mean.

Most of the patterns in this book are worked in a continuous spiral, so only join and make 1 chain if the pattern specifies it.

A useful tip - keep a notebook and pencil/pen close to hand to mark which rows you have completed, so they are easier to identify if you put your work down.

An asterisk * in a pattern means the start of a repeat. Repeat the pattern from the asterisk if the pattern instructs you to do this.

Other repeats are placed between square brackets with a note of how many times the instructions should be repeated. E.g. **[1 sc, 2 sc in next st] 6 times**, means work 1 sc in the next st, 2sc in the following st and repeat this whole set of instructions a total of 6 times.

At the end of rows or rounds where there has been a change in the stitch count, there will be a set of round brackets with the number of sts you should have on completion of this row or round, e.g. **(18 sts)**

Hook sizes

Crochet hooks come in all different shapes and sizes; bigger hooks make bigger stitches and smaller hooks make smaller stitches.

It is important to use the right hook size with the right yarn weight. This ensures you get the best possible outcome for your crochet work.

You can easily size up or down the projects in this book to make smaller or larger items. For example, use a 6-7mm hook and a super chunky yarn to crochet a Donut Buddy pillow. In the same way, use a smaller 2.5mm hook and sports weight yarn to produce a keyring or hanging ornament. The possibilities are endless!

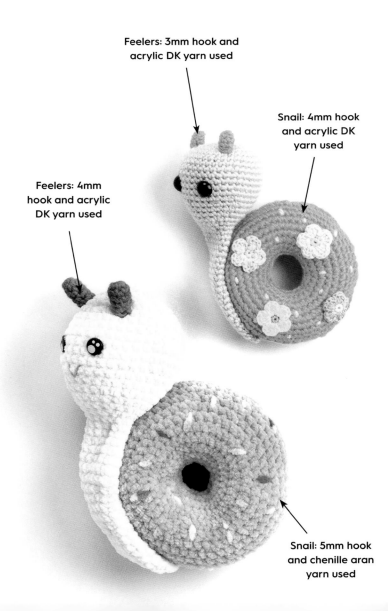

Feelers: 3mm hook and acrylic DK yarn used

Snail: 4mm hook and acrylic DK yarn used

Feelers: 4mm hook and acrylic DK yarn used

Snail: 5mm hook and chenille aran yarn used

Tools & Materials

Here is a list of everything you will need to make your Donut Buddies.

Crochet hooks

Crochet hooks are usually made of aluminium, plastic or wood. Metal hooks glide through the stitches easier. Choose a rubber or ergonomic handle for comfort. You will need sizes 2.5mm, 3mm and 4mm.

Stitch markers

You can use a variety of fun stitch markers, a strand of yarn in a contrasting colour or even a paperclip! Mark your last stitch of each round to make counting your stitches in each round easier.

Fibre fill stuffing

Fibre fill stuffing is usually made of polyester. It is soft and machine washable. Use the filling to stuff your Donut Buddies, creating a beautiful round shape, being careful not to overstuff your makes.

Safety eyes

Use black eyes from size 10mm up to size 14mm, unless otherwise stated. Pay attention to where you place them, as once you put the back on, they won't be able to be removed. Alternatively, you can embroider eyes (see **Basic Donut Pattern: Eyes**). Safety eyes are not recommended for small babies under three years old.

Scissors

Small pointed end scissors are the best things to use to snip away those little strands of yarn in hard to reach places.

Yarn or darning needle

Use your yarn needle to sew up your Donut Buddies and attach their facial features; you can use needles in different sizes and lengths for this.

Embroidery thread

You can use this thread to sew your donut characters together for a neater finish. Many donuts are decorated with thread as well.

Acrylic yarn

Acrylic DK (Double knit) or Worsted 4 weight yarn works better for older children (I use mainly Stylecraft Special DK/ Aran or Paintbox DK/Aran yarn).

Cotton yarn

4-ply or DK (double knit)/light worsted 3 weight yarn is perfect for smaller babies (I use mainly Scheepjes Soft Fun or Catona cotton yarn).

Pins

These are very handy to help keep the facial features in place while sewing them onto your Donut Buddies.

Rattle inserts

These come in various sizes. Size 1cm (½in) by 2cm (¾in) work best. Add up to three for a loud rattle sound.

Squeakers and jingly bells

These can be added inside a donut's ears, nose or body to create a fun sound.

Key chain clips

Use key chain clips to add to smaller cotton Donut Buddies to create hanging key chains and add them to your keys or bags for a fun accessory.

Safety Warning
Safety eyes are not recommended for children under three years. Leave out small accessories and hanging parts when gifting to small children.

Basic Donut Pattern

The majority of the patterns in this book are based on the Basic Donut pattern that follows. This is not repeated in the patterns, so turn back to this page to start each donut (unless specified). If you wish, you can add sprinkles to your icing or choose not to add them – make it your own!

YOU WILL NEED

- Size 4mm (US G/6) hook
- 50g (2oz) DK or worsted/Aran weight yarn in your chosen colours for the base and icing
- Donut making kit list

DONUT MAKING KIT LIST

In addition to hook and yarn, there are just a few things you'll need to complete the Basic Donut and all the Donut Buddies in this book, as listed here:

- Fibre fill stuffing
- Darning needle
- Scissors
- Stitch marker (optional)
- Rattle inserts, squeakers or bells for inside the donut, 10–15mm (⅜–⅝in) (optional)

Donut Buddies measure approximately 10–12.5cm (4–5in) wide depending on yarn weight and hook size used. See **How to Use This Book***.*

PATTERN ABBREVIATIONS

The patterns in this book are written using US crochet terms. These are listed here, along with their UK equivalents (where applicable). See **Crochet Techniques** for explanations and diagrams for all sts.

slst: slip stitch

yo: yarn over

ch: chain

rnd: round

st(s): stitch(es)

sc: single crochet (UK double crochet)

hdc: half double crochet (UK half-treble crochet)

dc: double crochet (UK treble crochet)

trc: treble crochet (UK double treble crochet)

inv dec: invisible decrease

hdc inv dec: half double crochet invisible decrease (UK half-treble crochet invisible decrease)

hdc3tog: half double crochet 3 together (UK half-treble crochet 3 together)

dc3tog: double crochet 3 together (UK treble crochet 3 together)

bs: bobble stitch

shs: shell stitch

blo: back loop only

rs: right side

ws: wrong side

DONUT BASE

1 ch at round 1 only; the donut base and icing patterns use the amigurumi method of working in a spiral without joining each round with a slst. It will help to use a stitch marker in the first st of the round so that you know when you have completed the round. Move the marker up as you work.

Using 4mm hook and your chosen yarn colour, make 20 ch; join into a circle with a slst.

Round 1: 1 ch; [1 sc back into the same st, 2 sc in next st] 10 times. (30 sts)

Round 2: 1 sc in each st around.

Round 3: [2 sc, 2 sc in next st] 10 times. (40 sts)

Round 4: 1 sc in each st around.

Round 5: [3 sc, 2 sc in next st] 10 times. (50 sts)

Rounds 6 to 11: 1 sc in each st around.

Round 12: [3 sc, inv dec] 10 times. (40 sts)

Round 13: 1 sc in each st around.

Round 14: [2 sc, inv dec] 10 times. (30 sts)

Round 15: 1 sc in each st around.

Round 16: [1 sc, inv dec] 10 times. (20 sts)

Slst in next st and fasten off. Cut yarn, leaving a long tail for sewing.

Fold the donut flat so that both holes are touching, sew closed working through both loops on each side of the hole, adding fibre fill stuffing a little at a time as you go. Add rattle inserts here should you wish to use them.

ICING

Using a 4mm hook and your chosen yarn colour, leaving a long tail for sewing, 20 ch; join the chain with a slst.

Rounds 1 to 5: Repeat rounds 1 to 5 of **Donut Base**.

Rounds 6 to 8: 1 sc in each st around. (50 sts)

Round 9: To create the icing drips, work in each successive st as follows.

Drip 1: 1 sc, 1 hdc, 1 dc, 1 trc, 1 dc, 1 hdc, 3 sc;

Drip 2: 1 hdc, 1 dc, 2 trc, 1 dc, 3 sc;

Drip 3: 1 hdc, 2 dc, 1 hdc, 3 sc;

Drip 4: 1 hdc, 1 dc, 2 trc, 1 dc, 1 hdc, 3 sc;

Drip 5: 1 hdc, 2 dc, 1 trc, 1 dc, 1 hdc, 3 sc;

Drip 6: 2 hdc, 3 dc, 3 sc.

Slst in next st and fasten off. Cut yarn, leaving a long tail for sewing.

If you wish to decorate your donut with sprinkles, do this *before* sewing the icing to the donut base (see **Sprinkles**). Sew the icing onto the donut base starting from the hole in the centre, then sew the edges of the icing to the edge of the donut to secure.

SPRINKLES

Using small amounts of your preferred yarn colours, use a darning needle to sew small sprinkle lines from the back to the front of the icing, as many as you wish in random directions. Pull yarn to the back and tie off.

EYES

Even the Basic Donut can be brought to life by simply adding a pair of eyes. All the Donut Buddy characters featured in this book have safety eyes fitted (see **Option 1**), but these should only be used for children aged three years and above. For babies and children under three years of age, either make crochet eyes and sew them on securely (see **Option 2**) or embroider eyes using black yarn or embroidery thread (see **Option 3**).

Option 1: Safety eyes

Generally, safety eyes are placed between rounds 4 and 5 of the icing before sewing it to the donut base. Make sure to securely fasten them at the back, following the manufacturer's instructions. Any variation on safety eye placement will be given in the individual pattern instructions.

Option 2: Crocheted eyes

It's easy to crochet eyes following this pattern. Make 2.

Using 2.5mm hook and black, make a magic ring (see **Crochet Techniques**).

Round 1: 4 sc into ring. (4 sts)

Slst in next st and fasten off, cutting yarn to leave a long tail for sewing each eye securely to the donut.

Option 3: Embroidered eyes

Using black yarn or embroidery thread, sew closed eyes across three sts, evenly spaced apart. To add eyelashes at the corner of the closed eye, form a sideways 'V' shape. Weave in thread ends.

Eye positioning

Whether you choose to use safety eyes or to crochet or embroider the eyes for your chosen Donut Buddy, the positioning will have a big part to play in creating the character. The characters in this book show just how different the effect can be by placing the eyes above, below or on either side of the centre hole. Use the photographs of the finished Donut Buddies to guide you on positioning the eyes.

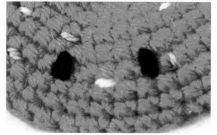

Highlight safety eyes by stitching a fleck of white embroidery thread on the outside edge of each eye.

Elephant

This adorable elephant is a firm favourite in the donut gang. A little rose accessorizes her frilly-edged ears beautifully (see **Accessories**), but you can omit this if you choose to.

YOU WILL NEED

- Size 2.5mm (US B/1 or C/2) and 4mm (US G/6) hooks
- DK or worsted/Aran weight yarn in light grey and dark grey
- Donut making kit list (see **Basic Donut Pattern**)
- Safety eyes, 2 x 10–14mm*, or black yarn or black embroidery thread to make your own

*Safety eyes should **only** be used for children aged three years or older.*

DONUT

Follow the **Basic Donut Pattern** to create the donut base in dark grey and the icing in light grey, omitting the sprinkles. If using safety eyes, place between rounds 4 and 5 of the icing before sewing it to the donut base, and securely fasten at the back following the manufacturer's instructions.

EARS (MAKE 2)

Using 4mm hook and light grey, make a magic ring.

Round 1: 6 sc into ring. (6 sts)

Round 2: 2 sc in each st around. (12 sts)

Round 3: [1 sc, 2 sc in next st] 6 times. (18 sts)

Round 4: [2 sc, 2 sc in next st] 6 times. (24 sts)

Round 5: [3 sc, 2 sc in next st] 6 times. (30 sts)

Round 6: [4 sc, 2 sc in next st] 6 times. (36 sts)

Round 7: [5 hdc, 2 hdc in next st] 6 times. (42 sts)

Round 8: *2 ch, 1 sc in next st; repeat from * until 10 sts remain.

Slst in next st and fasten off, leaving a long tail for sewing. Sew ears securely to back of donut with flat (un-frilled) edge attached to the donut base (see photo).

TRUNK

Using 2.5mm hook and light grey, make a magic ring.

Round 1: 4 sc into ring. (4 sts)

Round 2: 2 sc in each st around. (8 sts)

Rounds 3 to 8: 1 sc in each st around.

Round 9: 7 sc, 2 sc in next st. (9 sts)

Round 10: 2 sc in first st, 8 sc. (10 sts)

Round 11: 9 sc, 2 sc in next st. (11 sts)

Round 12: 2 sc in first st, 10 sc. (12 sts)

Slst in next st and fasten off, leaving a long tail for sewing. Lightly stuff the trunk and sew securely to the front of the donut, just under the hole, positioning it centrally between the eyes and bending it slightly upwards.

EYES

If using safety eyes, these will already have been placed when making the donut. Alternatively, to make the toy suitable for children under three years of age, you can crochet or embroider the eyes (see **Basic Donut Pattern: Eyes**).

FINISHING TOUCHES

To add a rose to your Elephant, make one in a colour of your choosing (see **Accessories**), then securely sew to the top corner of one of the ears.

After sewing the ears to the donut base, bend the ears to the front slightly to give them a nice curved shape.

Bunny

This sweet bunny rabbit makes a perfect spring gift. Add flowers and sprinkles to the ears to give her a fresh springtime feel, or leave these off if preferred.

YOU WILL NEED

- Size 4mm (US G/6) hook
- DK or worsted/Aran weight yarn in light purple and dark purple, plus small amounts of pink, yellow, pale blue and white
- Donut making kit list (see **Basic Donut Pattern**)
- Safety eyes, 2 x 10–14mm*, or black yarn or black embroidery thread to make your own

*Safety eyes should **only** be used for children aged three years or older.*

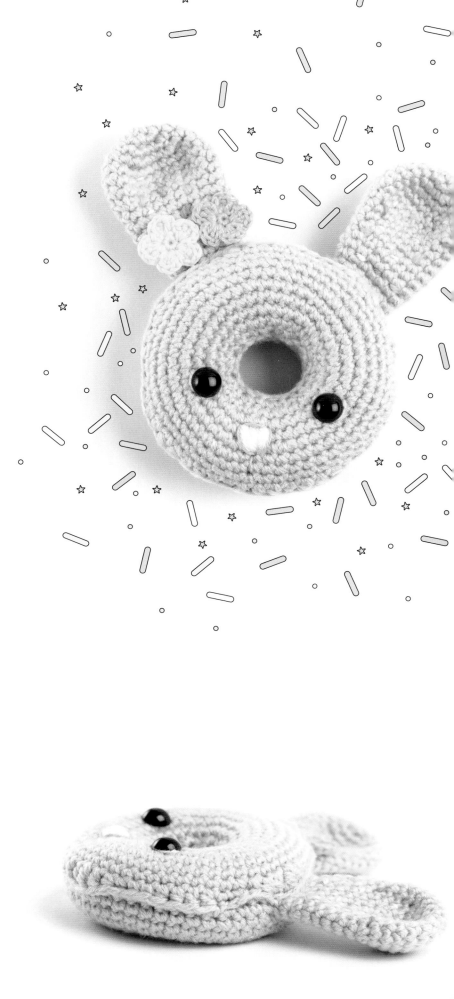

DONUT

Follow the **Basic Donut Pattern** to create the donut base in dark purple and the icing in light purple, omitting the sprinkles. If using safety eyes, place between rounds 4 and 5 of the icing before sewing it to the donut base, and securely fasten at the back following the manufacturer's instructions.

EARS (MAKE 2)

Using 4mm hook and light purple, make a magic ring.

Round 1: 6 sc into ring. (6 sts)

Round 2: 2 sc in each st around. (12 sts)

Round 3: [1 sc, 2 sc in next st] 6 times. (18 sts)

Round 4: [2 sc, 2 sc in next st] 6 times. (24 sts)

Rounds 5 to 7: 1 sc in each st around.

Round 8: [2 sc, inv dec] 6 times. (18 sts)

Rounds 9 to 11: 1 sc in each st around.

Round 12: [7 sc, inv dec] twice. (16 sts)

Round 13: 1 sc in each st around.

Round 14: [6 sc, inv dec] twice. (14 sts)

Round 15: 1 sc in each st around.

Fasten off, leaving a long tail for sewing.

Add sprinkles in yellow, pink and pale blue to front of ears (see **Basic Donut Pattern: Sprinkles**).

Sew ears securely to back of donut at top of donut hole, evenly spaced apart.

NOSE

Embroider a nose using white yarn below the donut hole, following the photo for guidance. Outline this with pink yarn, adding a vertical line below the nose.

EYES

If using safety eyes, these will already have been placed when making the donut. Alternatively, to make the toy suitable for children under three years of age, you can crochet or embroider the eyes (see **Basic Donut Pattern: Eyes**).

FINISHING TOUCHES

To add flowers to your Bunny, make one in yellow and one in pink (see **Accessories**), and sew securely to the bottom of one of the ears, overlapping them slightly.

Use a pastel colour palette for spring-themed donuts or make a more natural-coloured bunny with brown or grey yarn.

Owl

The donut family has many feathered friends, but with his wide-awake eyes and frilly chest feathers, the owl has to be one of the most popular in the gang. His friends think he's a hoot!

YOU WILL NEED

- Size 3mm (US C/2 or D/3) and 4mm (US G/6) hooks
- DK or worsted/Aran weight yarn in light blue and mid blue, plus small amounts of white and orange
- Donut making kit list (see **Basic Donut Pattern**)
- Safety eyes, 2 x 10–14mm*, or black yarn or black embroidery thread to make your own

*Safety eyes should **only** be used for children aged three years or older.*

DONUT

Follow the **Basic Donut Pattern** to create the donut base in mid blue and the icing in light blue, omitting the sprinkles.

EYE DISCS (MAKE 2)

Using 3mm hook and white, make a magic ring.

Round 1: 6 sc into ring. (6 sts)

Round 2: 2 sc in each st around. (12 sts)

Round 3: [1 sc, 2 sc in next st] 6 times. (18 sts)

Round 4: [2 sc, 2 sc in next st] 6 times. (24 sts)

Slst in next st and fasten off, leaving a long tail for sewing.

If using safety eyes, place in the centre of each eye disc and securely fasten at the back, following the manufacturer's instructions. If you prefer a sleepy owl, sew closed eyes with black yarn across the centre of the eye discs (see **Basic Donut Pattern: Eyes**). Sew the eye discs to the front of the donut, just above the hole and slightly overlapping them.

EARS (MAKE 2)

Using 3mm hook and light blue, make a magic ring.

Round 1: 4 sc into ring. (4 sts)

Round 2: [1 sc, 2 sc in next st] twice. (6 sts)

Round 3: 1 sc into each st around.

Round 4: [1 sc, 2 sc in next st] 3 times. (9 sts)

Round 5: [2 sc, 2 sc in next st] 3 times. (12 sts)

Round 6: [3 sc, 2 sc in next st] 3 times. (15 sts)

Fasten off, leaving a long tail for sewing. Securely sew ears to top of donut above the eye disks.

BEAK

Using 3mm hook and orange, make a magic ring.

Round 1: 4 sc into ring. (4 sts)

Round 2: [1 sc, 2 sc in next st] twice. (6 sts)

Round 3: [1 sc, 2 sc in next st] 3 times. (9 sts)

Rounds 4 to 5: 1 sc into each st around. (9 sts)

Fasten off, leaving a long tail for sewing. Lightly stuff the beak, then sew it centrally at the top of the donut hole where the eye discs meet.

WINGS (MAKE 2)

Using 4mm hook and light and mid blue, make a magic ring.

Round 1: 6 sc into ring. (6 sts)

Round 2: 2 sc in each st around. (12 sts)

Round 3: [1 sc, 2 sc in next st] 6 times. (18 sts)

Round 4: 9 sc, 1 ch, turn work, 1 sc in each of same 9 sts.

Fasten off, leaving a long tail for sewing. Securely sew top of wings to sides of donut across icing and donut base.

CHEST PANEL

Using 4mm hook and mid blue, make a magic ring.

Round 1: 6 sc into ring. (6 sts)

Round 2: 2 sc in each st around. (12 sts)

Round 3: [1 sc, 2 sc in next st] 6 times. (18 sts)

Round 4: [2 sc, 2 sc in next st] 6 times. (24 sts)

Round 5: [3 sc, 2 sc in next st] 6 times. (30 sts)

Round 6: 3 ch, 1 sc, *3 ch, 1 sc; repeat from * 4 more times.

Fasten off, leaving a long tail for sewing. Before attaching the chest panel to the donut, embroider sprinkles in light blue to create a pattern radiating out from the centre of the chest (see **Basic Donut Pattern: Sprinkles**).

Securely sew the chest to the bottom of the hole so that the frilly ends hang over the bottom of the donut, making sure that it is centred beneath the beak.

Horse

With her bright blue bridle and her well-groomed mane, this sweet little horse is eager to compete in her very first horse show. Let's cheer her on as she jumps for the crowd!

YOU WILL NEED

- Size 3mm (US C/2 or D/3) and 4mm (US G/6) hooks
- DK or worsted/Aran weight yarn in dark brown, plus small amounts of white, beige, turquoise blue and yellow
- Donut making kit list (see **Basic Donut Pattern**)
- Safety eyes, 2 x 10–14mm*, or black yarn or black embroidery thread to make your own

*Safety eyes should **only** be used for children aged three years or older.*

DONUT

Follow the **Basic Donut Pattern** to create the donut base and the icing in dark brown, omitting the sprinkles. If using safety eyes, place between rounds 4 and 5 of the icing before sewing it to the donut base, and securely fasten at the back following the manufacturer's instructions.

EARS (MAKE 2)

Using 4mm hook and dark brown, make a magic ring.

Round 1: 6 sc into ring. (6 sts)

Round 2: [2 sc, 2 sc in next st] twice. (8 sts)

Round 3: 1 sc in each st around.

Round 4: [1 sc, 2 sc in next st] 4 times. (12 sts)

Round 5: 1 sc in each st around.

Round 6: [1 sc, 2 sc in next st] 6 times. (18 sts)

Rounds 7 to 9: 1 sc in each st around.

Round 10: [Inv dec] 9 times. (9 sts)

Fasten off, leaving a long tail for sewing. Sew the ears at the top of the donut, evenly spaced, attached to the back of the icing.

FACE PANEL

The face panel is worked in rows.

Using 3mm hook and white, make 5 ch.

Row 1: Starting in second ch from the hook 1 sc in each st across, turn. (4 sts)

Row 2: 1 ch (does not count as st throughout), 1 sc in each st across, turn.

Row 3: 1 ch, 2 sc in first st, 2 sc, 2 sc in next st, turn. (6 sts)

Row 4: 1 ch, 1 sc in each st across, turn.

Row 5: 1 ch, [2 sc in next st, 1 sc] 3 times, turn. (9 sts)

Rows 6 to 7: 1ch. 1 sc in each st across, turn. (9 sts)

Row 8: 1 ch, [2 sc, 2 sc in next st] 3 times, turn. (12 sts)

Row 9: 1 ch, 1 sc in each st across, turn.

Row 10: [2 sc in first st, 3 sc] 3 times, turn. (15 sts)

Row 11: 1 sc in each st across.

Fasten off, leaving a long tail for sewing. Placing the face panel centrally between the ears, securely sew in place starting from the hole and working towards the edge of the donut.

MANE

(See **Crochet Techniques: Attaching the Hair** to see the basic technique for attaching the mane.)

Working between the ears, use a darning needle to thread small pieces of brown yarn from the back to the front of the icing, tying each in a secure knot. Trim secured yarn pieces to an even length, then brush or comb gently to create a frizzy look.

MUZZLE

Using 4mm hook and beige, make a magic ring.

Round 1: 6 sc into ring. (6 sts)

Round 2: 2 sc in each st around. (12 sts)

Round 3: [1 sc, 2 sc in next st] 6 times. (18 sts)

Round 4: [2 sc, 2 sc in next st] 6 times. (24 sts)

Round 5: [3 sc, 2 sc in next st] 6 times. (30 sts)

Rounds 6 to 8: 1 sc in each st around.

Fasten off, leaving a long tail for sewing. Lightly stuff the muzzle and securely sew it in the centre of the bottom of the donut. Referring to the photograph, sew two vertical lines for the nostrils using yellow yarn or embroidery thread.

EYES

If using safety eyes, these will already have been placed when making the donut. Alternatively, to make the toy suitable for children under three years of age, you can crochet or embroider the eyes (see **Basic Donut Pattern: Eyes**).

BRIDLE

The bridle is made of several parts: a noseband that wraps around the muzzle, 2 cheek pieces, and 2 rein studs that hide the join.

Noseband

Using a 3mm hook and turquoise blue, make 3 ch.

Row 1: 1 sc into second ch from hook, 1 sc, turn. (2 sts)

Row 2: 1 ch (does not count as st), 2 sc, turn.

Repeat Row 2 to desired length, making sure the noseband fits all the way around muzzle. Fasten off, leaving a long tail for sewing.

Cheekpieces (make 2)

Using a 3mm hook and turquoise blue, make 3 ch.

Row 1: 1 sc into second ch from hook, 1 sc, turn. (2 sts)

Row 2: 1 ch (does not count as st), 2 sc, turn.

Repeat Row 2 to desired length, ensuring the cheekpieces fit from the side of the muzzle to the edge of the donut.

Rein studs (make 2)

Using a 3mm hook and yellow, make as crocheted eyes (see **Basic Donut Pattern: Eyes**).

Securely sew the noseband around the muzzle, then sew the cheekpieces from the side of the muzzle to the edge of the donut, angling them slightly. Sew the rein studs where noseband and cheekpieces meet.

Alien

This Donut Buddy has travelled from a galaxy far, far away to join our little donut family, so be sure to give him a nice warm welcome.

YOU WILL NEED

- Size 3mm (US C/2 or D/3) and 4mm (US G/6) hooks

- DK or worsted/Aran weight yarn in light green, plus small amount of pink

- Donut making kit list (see **Basic Donut Pattern**)

- Safety eyes, 2 x 10–14mm*, or black yarn or black embroidery thread to make your own

*Safety eyes should **only** be used for children aged three years or older.

You can give your alien one antenna like mine, or two to make it your own, or leave it off altogether.

DONUT

Follow the **Basic Donut Pattern** to create the donut base and icing in light green, omitting the sprinkles. If using safety eyes, place between rounds 4 and 5 of the icing before sewing it to the donut base, and securely fasten at the back following the manufacturer's instructions.

EARS (MAKE 2)

Using 3mm hook and light green, make a magic ring.

Round 1: 3 sc into ring. (3 sts)

Round 2: 2 sc in each st around. (6 sts)

Round 3: 1 sc in each st around.

Round 4: [1 sc, 2 sc in next st] 3 times. (9 sts)

Round 5: 1 sc in each st around.

Round 6: [2 sc, 2 sc in next st] 3 times. (12 sts)

Round 7: 1 sc in each st around.

Round 8: [3 sc, 2 sc in next st] 3 times. (15 sts)

Round 9: 1 sc in each st around.

Round 10: [4 sc, 2 sc in next st] 3 times. (18 sts)

Round 11: 1 sc in each st around.

Round 12: [5 sc, 2 sc in next st] 3 times. (21 sts)

Round 13: 1 sc in each st around.

Round 14: [5 sc, inv dec] 3 times. (18 sts)

Round 15: [4 sc, inv dec] 3 times. (15 sts)

Round 16: [3 sc, inv dec] 3 times. (12 sts)

Slst in next st and fasten off, leaving a long tail for sewing. Securely sew ears to back of icing, positioning each just above the middle of the donut hole and making sure they are evenly spaced apart.

ANTENNA

Using 3mm hook and light green, make a magic ring.

Round 1: 4 sc into ring, slst in next st, 4 ch.

Fasten off, leaving a long tail for sewing. Securely sew the antenna in place so that it is centred in between the ears.

EYES

If using safety eyes, these will already have been placed when making the donut. Alternatively, to make the toy suitable for children under three years of age, you can crochet or embroider the eyes (see **Basic Donut Pattern: Eyes**).

CHEEKS (MAKE 2)

Using 3mm hook and pink, make as crocheted eyes (see **Basic Donut Pattern: Eyes**).

Securely sew on cheeks just below the eyes.

MOUTH

Using a darning needle and black or brown embroidery thread, sew a small smile below the eyes in line with the cheeks.

Goat

Every donut farmyard scene should have at least one little billy goat. There are lots of super features to keep your hands busy, including horns and a goatee, of course!

YOU WILL NEED

- Size 2.5mm (US B/1 or C/2) and 4mm (US G/6) hooks

- DK or worsted/Aran weight yarn in light grey and cream, plus small amount of brown

- Donut making kit list (see **Basic Donut Pattern**)

- Safety eyes, 2 x 10-14mm*, or black yarn or black embroidery thread to make your own

*Safety eyes should **only** be used for children aged three years or older.*

Make three goats in slightly different shades for a fun game of The Three Billy Goats Gruff! "Who's that trip-trapping over my bridge?"

DONUT

Follow the **Basic Donut Pattern** to create the donut base in cream and the icing in light grey, omitting the sprinkles. If using safety eyes, place them between rounds 4 and 5 of the icing before sewing it to the donut base, and securely fasten at the back following the manufacturer's instructions.

EARS (MAKE 2)

Using 2.5mm hook and light grey, make a magic ring.

Round 1: 6 sc into ring. (6 sts)

Round 2: [1 sc, 2 sc in next st] 3 times. (9 sts)

Round 3: [2 sc, 2 sc in next st] 3 times. (12 sts)

Round 4: [3 sc, 2 sc in next st] 3 times. (15 sts)

Round 5 to 7: 1 sc in each st around.

Round 8: [3 sc, inv dec] 3 times. (12 sts)

Slst in next st and fasten off, leaving a long tail for sewing.

Fold the ear in half and seam along the bottom edge. Pinch the inside edge of the seam between your fingers to create the ear shape and sew a couple of sts to hold.

Referring to the photo of the finished donut, securely sew an ear to each side so that they are angled downwards.

HORNS (MAKE 2)

Using 2.5mm hook and cream, make a magic ring.

Round 1: 4 sc into ring. (4 sts)

Round 2: [1 sc, 2 sc in next st] twice. (6 sts)

Rounds 3 to 5: 1 sc in each st around.

Slst in next st and fasten off, leaving a long tail for sewing.

Lightly stuff the horns and securely sew them along the top edge of the donut above the ears, spacing them approximately 9 sts apart.

MUZZLE

Using 2.5mm hook and cream, make a magic ring.

Round 1: 6 sc into ring. (6 sts)

Round 2: 2 sc in each st around. (12 sts)

Round 3: [1 sc, 2 sc in next st] 6 times. (18 sts)

Round 4: [2 sc, 2 sc in next st] 6 times. (24 sts)

Rounds 5 to 7: 1 sc in each st around.

Slst in next st and fasten off, leaving a long tail for sewing.

To make a beard along the bottom edge of the muzzle, you will need a darning needle and small pieces of cream and light grey yarn (see **Crochet Techniques: Attaching the Hair** to see the basic technique for attaching the beard). Weave each piece of yarn in from the back of the muzzle to the front, wrap around to the front once more, then pull through to the back and securely fasten. Trim secured yarn pieces to an even length and slightly fray the ends.

Using brown yarn, embroider a small nose and mouth line on the muzzle.

Lightly stuff the muzzle and securely sew it to the bottom half of the donut, lining up the mouth line with the centre point of the hole.

EYES

If using safety eyes, these will already have been placed when making the donut. Alternatively, to make the toy suitable for children under three years of age, you can crochet or embroider the eyes (see **Basic Donut Pattern: Eyes**).

Sun

The sun is always shining in donut land, and with her super cheerful disposition, this Donut Buddy is sure to brighten up even the dullest of days.

YOU WILL NEED

- Size 2.5mm (US B/1 or C/2) and 4mm (US G/6) hooks

- DK or worsted/Aran weight yarn in egg yolk yellow and bright yellow, plus small amounts of bright pink and mid pink

- Donut making kit list (see **Basic Donut Pattern**)

- Safety eyes, 2 x 10–14mm*, or black yarn or black embroidery thread to make your own

*Safety eyes should **only** be used for children aged three years or older.

Use a smaller or larger hook as necessary to create sun rays the right size to fit 10 around the edge of your donut.

DONUT

Follow the **Basic Donut Pattern** to create the donut base in egg yolk yellow and the icing in bright yellow, omitting the sprinkles. If using safety eyes, place between rounds 4 and 5 of the icing before sewing it to the donut base, and securely fasten at the back following the manufacturer's instructions.

SUN RAYS (MAKE 5 OF EACH COLOUR)

Using 2.5mm hook and egg yolk yellow or bright yellow, make a magic ring.

Round 1: 4 sc into ring. (4 sts)

Round 2: [1 sc, 2 sc in next st] twice. (6 sts)

Round 3: [2 sc, 2 sc in next st] twice. (8 sts)

Round 4: [3 sc, 2 sc in next st] twice. (10 sts)

Round 5: [4 sc, 2 sc in next st] twice. (12 sts)

Round 6: [2 sc in next st, 1 sc] 6 times. (18 sts)

Rounds 7 to 8: 1 sc in each st around.

Slst in next st and fasten off, leaving a long tail for sewing.

Lightly stuff the sun rays and securely sew them around the edge of the donut, alternating colours.

EYES

If using safety eyes, these will already have been placed when making the donut. Alternatively, to make the toy suitable for children under three years of age, you can crochet or embroider the eyes (see **Basic Donut Pattern: Eyes**).

CHEEKS (MAKE 2)

Using 2.5mm hook and bright pink, make as crocheted eyes (see **Basic Donut Pattern: Eyes**). Securely sew the cheeks just below and to the side of the eyes.

FINISHING TOUCHES

Use the mid pink yarn to sew a small V-shaped smile line centrally spaced between the eyes just below the cheeks.

Highlight safety or crochet eyes by adding 3 straight line sts radiating out from the corner of each eye for the eyelashes.

Hippo

No visit to the Donut Buddy zoo would be complete without saying "How do you do?" to our beautiful hippo. Instructions for making her sweet little bow can be found in **Accessories**.

YOU WILL NEED

- Size 2.5mm (US B/1 or C/2), 3mm (US C/2 or D/3) and 4mm (US G/6) hook

- DK or worsted/Aran weight yarn in blue-violet and mid purple, plus small amount of pink

- Donut making kit list (see **Basic Donut Pattern**)

- Safety eyes, 2 x 10–14mm*, or black yarn or black embroidery thread to make your own

*Safety eyes should **only** be used for children aged three years or older.*

To give your hippo more expression, you could embroider a smile at the base of the muzzle or add some eyelashes (see Sun Finishing Touches).

DONUT

Follow the **Basic Donut Pattern** to create the donut base in blue-violet and the icing in mid purple, omitting the sprinkles. If using safety eyes, place between rounds 4 and 5 of the icing before sewing it to the donut base, and securely fasten at the back following the manufacturer's instructions.

EARS (MAKE 2)

Using 2.5mm hook and pink for inner ear, make a magic ring.

Round 1: 6 sc into ring. (6 sts)

Slst in next st, fasten off and weave in ends.

Using mid purple for outer ear, continue as follows.

Round 2: 2 sc in each st around. (12 sts)

Round 3: [1 sc, 2 sc in next st] 6 times. (18 sts)

Slst in next st and fasten off, leaving a long tail for sewing. At the fastened off end of each ear, pinch between your fingers to make a curved shape and sew closed across 3 sts to retain the shape. Referring to the photo of the finished donut and working at the back of the icing, sew on ears, spacing them evenly apart.

MUZZLE

Work around both sides of the foundation chain in round 1 and continuously in rounds from end round 2.

Using a 3mm hook and mid purple, make 8 ch.

Round 1: 1 sc in 2nd ch from hook and in next 5 sts, 3 sc in last st. Working into other side of foundation ch, 5 sc, 2 sc in last st, slst in next st. (16 sts)

Round 2: 1 ch (does not count as a st), 2 sc in first st, 5 sc, 2 sc in next st, 1 sc in next st, 2 sc in next st, 5 sc, 2 sc in next st, 1 sc. (20 sts)

Round 3: 2 sc in first st, 7 sc, 2 sc in next st, 1 sc, 2 sc in next st, 7 sc, 2 sc in next st, 1 sc. (24 sts)

Round 4: 1 sc, 2 sc in next 2 sts, 6 sc, 2 sc in next 2 sts, 2 sc, 2 sc in next 2 sts, 6 sc, 2 sc in next 2 sts, 1 sc. (32 sts)

Round 5: Working into blo, 1 sc in each st around.

Rounds 6 to 8: 1 sc in each st around.

Slst in next st and fasten off, leaving a long tail for sewing. Lightly stuff the muzzle and securely sew in the centre of the bottom of the donut. Referring to the photograph, embroider the nostrils using muzzle yarn.

EYES

If using safety eyes, these will already have been placed when making the donut. Alternatively, to make the toy suitable for children under three years of age, you can crochet or embroider the eyes (see **Basic Donut Pattern: Eyes**).

FINISHING TOUCHES

To add a bow to your hippo, make one in pink (see **Accessories**), then sew securely to bottom of one of the ears.

Tiger

Here's a chance to perfect your yarn embroidery skills to capture the symmetry of this little tiger's spectacular stripes. But don't be afraid, he's just a big pussycat!

YOU WILL NEED

- Size 3mm (US C/2 or D/3) and 4mm (US G/6) hooks

- DK or worsted/Aran weight yarn in black, orange and white

- Donut making kit list (see **Basic Donut Pattern**)

- Safety eyes, 2 x 10–14mm*, or black yarn or black embroidery thread to make your own

*Safety eyes should **only** be used for children aged three years or older.*

I have made the V-shaped lines just beneath the tiger's eyes twice as thick as the other stripes to define the face shape.

DONUT

Follow the **Basic Donut Pattern** to create the donut base in black and icing in orange, omitting the sprinkles. If using safety eyes, place between rounds 4 and 5 of the icing before sewing it to the donut base, and securely fasten at the back following the manufacturer's instructions.

EARS (MAKE 2)

Using 4mm hook and orange, make a magic ring.

Round 1: 6 sc into ring. (6 sts)

Round 2: [2 sc, 2 sc in next st] twice. (8 sts)

Round 3: 1 sc in each st around.

Round 4: [1 sc, 2 sc in next st] 4 times. (12 sts)

Round 5: 1 sc in each st around.

Round 6: [1 sc, 2 sc in next st] 6 times. (18 sts)

Round 7: 1 sc in each st around.

Slst in next st and fasten off, leaving a long tail for sewing.

Using white yarn, embroider 3 long sts to define the shape of the ear. Work from the same point at the top of the ear through front of ear only; fasten off from the inside to hide yarn ends.

Referring to the photo of the finished donut, securely sew an ear to each side, evenly spaced apart.

MUZZLE

Using 3mm hook and white, make a magic ring.

Round 1: 6 sc into ring. (6 sts)

Round 2: 2 sc in each st around. (12 sts)

Round 3: [1 sc, 2 sc in next st] 6 times. (18 sts)

Round 4: 5 sc, 3 sc in next st, 7 sc, 3 sc in next st, 4 sc. (22 sts)

Rounds 5 to 6: 1 sc in each st around.

Slst in next st and fasten off, leaving a long tail for sewing.

Using black yarn, embroider a nose and mouth on the muzzle. Start by defining the shape of the nose, outlining a triangle from the middle of the muzzle approx. 3 rounds deep and 6 sts wide. Weave the yarn back and forth to completely fill the nose shape, then sew a straight line beneath for the mouth.

Lightly stuff the muzzle and securely sew it to the bottom half of the donut, lining up the mouth line with the centre point of the hole.

EYES

If using safety eyes, these will already have been placed when making the donut. Alternatively, to make the toy suitable for children under three years of age, you can crochet or embroider the eyes (see **Basic Donut Pattern: Eyes**).

STRIPES

Referring to the photo of the finished donut as your guide, embroider the tiger's stripes using black yarn.

Chicken

This cute chicken is always up at the break of dawn. You'll need to perfect the shell stitch to complete her, as her icing is just a little different from the norm.

YOU WILL NEED

- Size 2.5mm (US B/1 or C/2), 3mm (US C/2 or D/3) and 4mm (US G/6) hooks
- DK or worsted/Aran weight yarn in cream, yellow and red
- Donut making kit list (see **Basic Donut Pattern**)
- Safety eyes, 2 x 10–14mm*, or black yarn or black embroidery thread to make your own

*Safety eyes should **only** be used for children aged three years or older.*

DONUT BASE

Follow the **Basic Donut Pattern** to create the donut base in cream.

ICING

Using 4mm hook and cream, work as standard icing to end of round 8.

Rounds 1 to 8: Repeat rounds 1 to 8 of standard icing (see **Basic Donut Pattern: Icing**).

Round 9: [5 dc in next st (makes shs), skip next st, slst in next st] 6 times. (6 shell sts)

Slst in next st, fasten off, leaving long tail for sewing.

If using safety eyes, place between rounds 6 and 7 of the icing before sewing to the donut base, and securely fasten at the back following the manufacturer's instructions.

Sew the icing to the donut base starting at the hole, then sew around the edge.

COMB (MAKE 3)

Using 3mm hook and red, make a magic ring.

Round 1: 6 sc into ring. (6 sts)

Rounds 2 to 4: 1 sc in each st around.

Slst in next st and fasten off, leaving a long tail for sewing. Lightly stuff each piece, then securely sew in a line, centring them between the eyes, one in front of the other.

EYES

If using safety eyes, these will already have been placed when making the icing. Alternatively, to make the toy suitable for children under three years of age, you can crochet or embroider the eyes (see **Basic Donut Pattern: Eyes**). Use red yarn to embroider a long st diagonally beneath each eye.

BEAK

Using 3mm hook and yellow, make a magic ring.

Round 1: 4 sc into ring. (4 sts)

Round 2: [1 sc, 2 sc in next st] twice. (6 sts)

Round 3: [1 sc, 2 sc in next st] 3 times. (9 sts)

Rounds 4 to 5: 1 sc in each st around.

Slst in next st and fasten off, leaving a long tail for sewing. Lightly stuff the beak, then securely sew to the centre top of the donut hole beneath the eyes.

WINGS (MAKE 2)

Using 3mm hook and cream, make a magic ring.

Round 1: 6 sc into ring. (6 sts)

Round 2: 2 sc in each st around. (12 sts)

Round 3: [1 sc, 2 sc in next st] 6 times. (18 sts)

Round 4: 4 ch, 1 sc in next st, 4 ch, 1 sc into same st, 1 sc in next st, 4 ch, 1 sc in next st, 4 ch, 1 sc into same st, slst into the next st.

Fasten off, leaving a long tail for sewing. Securely sew wings on at each side, with half of the wing attached to the icing and half attached to the donut base.

WATTLE (MAKE 2)

Using 2.5mm hook and red, make a magic ring.

Round 1: 4 sc into ring. (4 sts)

Rounds 2 to 3: 1 sc in each st around.

Fasten off, leaving a long tail for sewing. Lightly stuff each piece, then securely sew on behind the beak; fasten off at back of donut.

FEET (MAKE 2)

Each foot has 3 toes. The first 2 toes are made separately, then joined to make a foot as the third toe is completed.

For first 2 toes

Using 2.5mm hook and yellow, make a magic ring.

Round 1: 6 sc into ring. (6 sts)

Rounds 2 to 5: 1 sc in each st around.

Slst in next st, fasten off and weave in ends.

For third toe

Repeat rounds 1 to 5 but do not fasten off; continue to make foot.

Round 6: Pulling the toe on the hook together with one of the fastened off toes, sc in first 2 sts around, making sure to catch both loops of the toe to join; 1 sc in next st along, bringing the third toe together, sc in next 2 sts making sure to catch both loops of the toe to join; 9 sc. (18 sts)

Rounds 7 to 8: 1 sc in each st around.

Slst in next st and fasten off, leaving a long tail for sewing. Lightly stuff the feet, working a little stuffing into the toes. Securely sew the feet behind the icing at the bottom edge of the donut, allowing a little space in between.

Zebra

This stripy fella loves running around in the wild. He also loves meeting up with his Donut Buddy pals for a bit of fun. His cute stripes and triangles can be made in varying sizes.

YOU WILL NEED

- Size 3mm (US C/2 or D/3) and 4mm (US G/6) hooks
- DK or worsted/Aran weight yarn in white and black
- Donut making kit list (see **Basic Donut Pattern**)
- Safety eyes, 2 x 10–14mm*, or black yarn or black embroidery thread to make your own

*Safety eyes should **only** be used for children aged three years or older.*

DONUT

Follow the **Basic Donut Pattern** to create the donut base in black and the icing in white, omitting the sprinkles. If using safety eyes, place between rounds 4 and 5 of the icing.

EARS (MAKE 2)

Using 3mm hook and white, make a magic ring.

Round 1: 6 sc into ring. (6 sts)

Round 2: [1 sc, 2 sc in next st] 3 times. (9 sts)

Change to black.

Round 3: 1 sc, [2 sc in next st, 2 sc] twice, 2 sc in next st, 1 sc. (12 sts)

Round 4: [3 sc, 2 sc in next st] 3 times. (15 sts)

Change to white.

Round 5: 2 sc, 2 sc in next st, [4 sc, 2 sc in next st] twice, 2 sc. (18 sts)

Round 6: [5 sc, 2 sc in next st] 3 times. (21 sts)

Change to black.

Round 7: 1 sc in each st around. (21 sts)

Round 8: [5 sc, inv dec] 3 times. (18 sts)

Change to white.

Round 9: 2 sc, inv dec, [4 sc, inv dec] twice, 2 sc. (15 sts)

Round 10: [3 sc, inv dec] 3 times. (12 sts)

Round 11: 1 sc in each st around.

Slst in next st, fasten off, cut yarn, leaving a long tail for sewing. Sew ears on each side of the donut hole, at the back of the icing, evenly spaced apart.

MUZZLE

Using 3mm hook and black, make a magic ring.

Round 1: 6 sc into ring. (6 sts)

Round 2: 2 sc in each st around. (12 sts)

Round 3: [1 sc, 2 sc in next st] 6 times. (18 sts)

Round 4: [2 sc, 2 sc in next st] 6 times. (24 sts)

Round 5: [3 sc, 2 sc in next st] 6 times. (30 sts)

Rounds 6 to 8: 1 sc in each st around.

Slst in next st, fasten off, cut yarn, leaving a long tail for sewing. Lightly stuff and sew the muzzle central to the donut ring hole, adding two nostril lines with white yarn.

EYES

If using safety eyes, these will already have been placed when making the donut. Alternatively, to make the toy suitable for children under three years of age, you can crochet or embroider the eyes (see **Basic Donut Pattern: Eyes**), placing the eyes just above the muzzle. Add eyelashes and a thin black line around the top of the eye using black embroidery thread to create a hooded eye effect.

MANE

(See **Crochet Techniques: Attaching the Hair** to see the basic technique for attaching the mane.)

Cut as many strands of black and white yarn as you wish, roughly 5cm in length, and thread them from the back of the icing to the front, making sure to knot the back tightly. Place evenly between the ears and trim to 2.5cm in length.

STRIPES

Using 3mm hook and black, crochet as many ch as you would like to fit across your Donut Buddy; see below for a guide.

Large Stripes (make 2)
Make a ch of between 12 to 15 sts (depending on tension). Fasten off and cut yarn, leaving a long tail for sewing.

Medium Stripes (make 2)
Make a ch of between 10 to 12 sts (depending on tension), fasten off, cut yarn, leaving a long tail for sewing.

TRIANGLES

Using 3mm hook and black, crochet the following triangles to the size you prefer.

Large Triangles (make 3)
Using 3mm hook and black, make 6 ch.

Row 1: sc in 2nd ch from the hook and in each st across, turn. (5 sts)

Row 2: 1 ch (does not count as st throughout), 1 sc, inv dec, 2 sc, turn. (4 sts)

Row 3: 1 ch, 1 sc, inv dec, 1 sc, turn. (3 sts)

Row 4: 1 ch, 1 sc, inv dec, turn. (2 sts)

Row 5: 1 ch, inv dec, fasten off, cut yarn leaving a long tail for sewing. (1 st)

Small Triangles (make 2)
Using 3mm hook and black, make 4 ch.

Row 1: slst in the 2nd ch from the hook, 1 hdc, 1 dc, fasten off, cut yarn, leaving a long tail for sewing.

Sew the Zebra stripes and triangles onto the face, placing the stripes and triangles however you choose.

Chameleon

With his beautiful orange fingers and toes and bright blue frill, why would this colourful Donut Buddy ever want to blend in? Use a mixture of vibrant colours to bring him to life!

YOU WILL NEED

- Size 2.5mm (US B/1), 3mm (US C/2 or D/3) and 4mm (US G/6) hooks

- DK or worsted/Aran weight yarn in beige, lime, shrimp, bright pink and turquoise

- Embroidery thread in pink, lime and blue

- Donut making kit list (see **Basic Donut Pattern**)

- Safety eyes, 2 x 10–14mm*, or black yarn or black embroidery thread to make your own

*Safety eyes should **only** be used for children aged three years or older.*

DONUT

Follow the **Basic Donut Pattern** to create the donut base in beige and the icing in lime, omitting the sprinkles.

HEAD

Using 3mm hook and lime, make a magic ring.

Round 1: 8 sc into ring. (8 sts)

Round 2: 3 sc in the first st, 3 sc, 3 sc in next st, 3 sc. (12 sts)

Round 3: 1 sc, 3 sc in next st, 5 sc, 3 sc in next st, 4 sc. (16 sts)

Round 4: 2 sc, 3 sc in next st, 7 sc, 3 sc in next st, 5 sc. (20 sts)

Round 5: 3 sc, 3 sc in next st, 9 sc, 3 sc in next st, 6 sc. (24 sts)

Rounds 6 to 7: 1 sc in each st around.

Round 8: 8 sc, 2 sc in the next 6 sts, 10 sc. (30 sts)

Round 9: 8 sc, [1 sc, 2 sc in next st] 6 times, 10 sc. (36 sts)

Rounds 10 to 14: 1 sc in each st around.

Round 15: 12 sc, inv dec, 8 sc, inv dec, 12 sc. (34 sts)

Rounds 16 to 18: 1 sc in each st around.

2 slst, fasten off, cut yarn, leaving a long tail for sewing. Lightly stuff, then sew the head at one side of the donut.

EYES (MAKE 2)

Using 2.5mm hook and lime, make a magic ring.

Round 1: 8 sc in a magic ring. If using safety eyes, place one in the centre of the ring and pull tightly, making sure to fasten the eye securely from the back. (8 sts)

Alternatively, to make the toy suitable for children under three years of age, you can crochet or embroider the eyes (see **Basic Donut Pattern: Eyes**). Sew either open or closed eyes in the centre of the eye.

Rounds 2 to 3: 1 sc in each st around.

Round 4: 2 sc in each st around. (16 sts)

Round 5: 1 sc in each st around.

Change to bright pink.

Round 6: 1 sc in each st around, slst in next st, fasten off, cut yarn, leaving a long tail for sewing. Lightly stuff and sew eyes on each side of the head.

FRILL

Using 2.5mm hook and turquoise, starting in the 6th or 7th row of the head closest to the donut body, insert the hook through a st [A] and attach the yarn, 1 ch to secure, 1 sc back in the same st [B], 1 sc in the next row along, 1 ch, 1 sc back in the same st, repeat all the way down the back of the head [C] and the edge of the icing along the back of the chameleon for as long as you wish [D], fasten off and weave in ends.

MOUTH

Take a small about of your preferred colour yarn and a darning needle and sew a small smile line through the bottom of the head just below the eyes, fasten off and weave in ends.

ARM (MAKE 2)

First Finger
Using 2.5mm hook and shrimp, make a magic ring.

Round 1: 4 sc into ring. (4 sts)

Rounds 2 to 3: 1 sc in each st around.

Slst in next st, fasten off and weave in ends.

Second Finger
Using 2.5mm hook and shrimp, make a magic ring.

Round 1: 4 sc into ring. (4 sts)

Rounds 2 to 4: 1 sc in each st around.

Round 5: Bring both fingers together and slst to join, 1 sc back in the same st, 1 sc in each st around. (8 sts)

Change to lime.

Rounds 6 to 8: 1 sc in each st around.

Slst in next st, fasten off, cut yarn, leaving a long tail for sewing. Lightly stuff, then sew onto body.

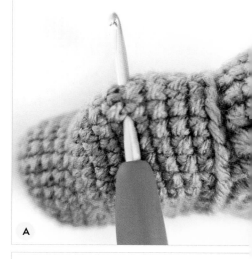

LEGS (MAKE 2)

Using 2.5mm hook and shrimp, make a magic ring.

First Toe

Round 1: 4 sc into ring. (4 sts)

Rounds 2 to 3: 1 sc in each st around.

Slst in next st, fasten off and weave in ends.

Second Toe

Round 1: 4 sc into ring. (4 sts)

Rounds 2 to 4: 1 sc in each st around.

Round 5: Bring both toes together and slst to join, 1 sc back in the same st, 1 sc in each st around. (8 sts)

Round 6: 1 sc in each st around.

Change to lime.

Round 7: 2 sc in the first st, 3 sc, 2 sc in next st, 3 sc. (10 sts)

Rounds 8 to 9: 1 sc in each st around.

Slst in next st, fasten off, cut yarn, leaving a long tail for sewing. Lightly stuff, then sew legs onto body.

TAIL

Using 2.5mm hook and lime, make a magic ring.

Round 1: 5 sc into ring. (5 sts)

Rounds 2 to 3: 1 sc in each st around.

Round 4: 2 sc in the first st, 4 sc. (6 sts)

Rounds 5 to 6: 1 sc in each st around.

Round 7: 2 sc in the first st, 5 sc. (7 sts)

Round 8: 1 sc in each st around.

Round 9: 2 sc in the first st, 6 sc. (8 sts)

Rounds 10 to 12: 1 sc in each st around.

Round 13: 2 sc in the first st, 7 sc. (9 sts)

Rounds 14 to 16: 1 sc in each st around.

Round 17: 2 sc in the first st, 8 sc. (10 sts)

Rounds 18 to 19: 1 sc in each st around.

Round 20: 2 sc in the first st, 9 sc. (11 sts)

Rounds 21 to 22: 1 sc in each st around.

Round 23: 2 sc in the first st, 10 sc. (12 sts)

Rounds 24 to 25: 1 sc in each st around.

Round 26: 2 sc in the first st, 11 sc. (13 sts)

Round 27: 1 sc in each st around.

Round 28: 2 sc in the first st, 12 sc. (14 sts)

Round 29: 1 sc in each st around.

Round 30: 2 sc in the first st, 13 sc. (15 sts)

Rounds 31 to 32: 1 sc in each st around.

Slst in next st, fasten off, cut yarn, leaving a long tail for sewing. Lightly stuff top part of tail and sew to the other end of the donut, making sure not to over stuff.

BODY STRIPES

Using different coloured embroidery threads and working through from the front to the back with a darning needle, make small triangle shapes along the length of the chameleon's upper body, fasten off and weave in ends.

Turtle

This little buddy may be slow off the mark but he always gets to where he's going eventually. Instructions for making his flowers can be found in **Accessories**.

YOU WILL NEED

- Size 3mm (US C/2 or D/3) and 4mm (US G/6) hooks

- DK or worsted/Aran weight yarn in stone, mocha and grass green

- 4-ply cotton yarn in lavender and lemonade

- Donut making kit list (see **Basic Donut Pattern**)

- Safety eyes, 2 x 10–14mm*, or black yarn or black embroidery thread to make your own

*Safety eyes should **only** be used for children aged three years or older.*

Add as many flowers as you would like to the back of the donut to make it your own or leave them off completely.

DONUT

Follow the **Basic Donut Pattern** to create the donut base in stone, the icing in mocha and the sprinkles in lavender and lemonade.

HEAD

Using 4mm hook and grass green, make a magic ring.

Round 1: 6 sc into ring. (6 sts)

Round 2: 2 sc in each st around. (12 sts)

Round 3: [1 sc, 2 sc in next st] 6 times. (18 sts)

Round 4: [2 sc, 2 sc in next st] 6 times. (24 sts)

Rounds 5 to 8: 1 sc in each st around.

Round 9: [2 sc, inv dec] 6 times. (18 sts)

Round 10: [1 sc, inv dec] 6 times. (12 sts)

Slst in next st, fasten off, cut yarn and leave a long tail for sewing. Stuff the head and sew to the body central to the donut ring hole after adding the eyes. Add a smile using either yarn or embroidery thread.

LEGS (MAKE 4)

Using 3mm hook and grass green, make a magic ring.

Round 1: 6 sc into ring. (6 sts)

Round 2: 2 sc in each st around. (12 sts)

Rounds 3 to 6: 1 sc in each st around.

Slst in next st, fasten off, cut yarn leaving a long tail for sewing. Lightly stuff and attach legs, evenly spaced apart, on each side of the donut.

TAIL

Using 3mm hook and grass green, make a magic ring.

Round 1: 4 sc into ring. (4 sts)

Round 2: [1 sc, 2 sc in next st] twice. (6 sts)

Round 3: [2 sc, 2 sc in next st] twice. (8 sts)

Rounds 4 to 5: 1 sc in each st around.

Slst in next st, fasten off, cut yarn and leave a long tail for sewing. Lightly stuff the tail and attach to the donut, directly opposite the head.

EYES

If using safety eyes, place them between rounds 6 and 7 of the head, evenly spaced apart, and add white embroidery thread around one half of the eye. Alternatively, to make the toy suitable for children under three years of age, you can crochet or embroider the eyes (see **Basic Donut Pattern: Eyes**).

FINISHING TOUCHES

To add flowers to your turtle, make three in colours of your choice (see **Accessories**), then sew securely to one side of the turtle shell.

Sheep

Here's a chance to practise making bobbles for the face of this sweet cutie pie. With her lovely turned-down ears, she makes a pretty picture. Add a flower to complete her outfit.

YOU WILL NEED

- Size 3mm (US C/2 or D/3) and 4mm (US G/6) hooks
- DK or worsted/Aran weight yarn in parchment, cream and grey
- Embroidery thread in grey (optional)
- Donut making kit list (see **Basic Donut Pattern**)
- Safety eyes, 2 x 10–14mm*, or black yarn or black embroidery thread to make your own

*Safety eyes should **only** be used for children aged three years or older.*

DONUT BASE

Follow the **Basic Donut Pattern** to create the donut base in parchment.

ICING

Using 4mm hook and cream, leaving a long tail for sewing, make 20 ch, join to first ch to make a circle. (20 sts)

Round 1: 1 ch, 1 sc in the same st, 2 sc in next st, [1 sc, 2 sc in next st] 9 times. (30 sts)

Round 2: 15 sc, BS (bobble) in next st (see **Crochet Techniques**), [2 sc, BS] 4 times, 2 sc. (30 sts including 5 BS)

Round 3: [2 sc, 2 sc in next st] 10 times. (40 sts)

Round 4: 22 sc, BS, [1 sc, BS] 7 times, 3 sc. (40 sts including 8 BS)

Round 5: [3 sc, 2 sc in next st] 10 times. (50 sts)

Round 6: 28 sc, BS, [1 sc, BS] 9 times, 3 sc. (50 sts including 10 BS)

Rounds 7 to 8: sc in each st around.

In the next round, create 6 icing drips by working in each st as described.

Round 9: (Drip 1) 1 sc, 1 hdc, 1 dc, 1 trc, 1 dc, 1 hdc, 3 sc; (drip 2) 1 hdc, 1 dc, 2 trc, 1 dc, 3 sc; (drip 3) 1 hdc, 2 dc, 1 hdc, 3 sc; (drip 4) 1 hdc, 1 dc, 2 trc, 1 dc, 1 hdc, 3 sc; (drip 5) 1 hdc, 2 dc, 1 trc, 1 dc, 1 hdc, 3 sc; (drip 6) 2 hdc, 3 dc, 3 sc. (50 sts)

Slst in next st, fasten off, cut yarn, leaving a long tail for sewing together. Push bobbles back through to the right side of the icing. If using safety eyes, place them between rounds 4 and 5 of the icing before sewing to donut base. Sew icing to the donut starting from the small hole in the centre, then sew edges of the icing to the donut to secure.

MUZZLE

Using 3mm hook and grey, make a magic ring.

Round 1: 6 sc into ring. (6 sts)

Round 2: 2 sc in each st around. (12 sts)

Round 3: [1 sc, 2 sc in next st] 6 times. (18 sts)

Round 4: [2 sc, 2 sc in next st] 6 times. (24 sts)

Round 5: [3 sc, 2 sc in next st] 6 times. (30 sts)

Rounds 6 to 8: 1 sc in each st around.

Slst in next st, fasten off, cut yarn, leaving a long tail for sewing. Lightly stuff and attach muzzle central to donut ring hole on the flat part of the icing, adding nostril lines with grey yarn or embroidery thread.

EYES

If using safety eyes, these will already have been placed when making the donut. Alternatively, to make the toy suitable for children under three years of age, you can crochet or embroider the eyes (see **Basic Donut Pattern: Eyes**).

EARS (MAKE 2)

Using 3mm hook and grey, make a magic ring.

Round 1: 6 sc into ring. (6 sts)

Round 2: 2 sc in each st around. (12 sts)

Round 3: [1 sc, 2 sc in next st] 6 times. (18 sts)

Round 4: [2 sc, 2 sc in next st] 6 times. (24 sts)

Rounds 5 to 7: 1 sc in each st around.

Round 8: [2 sc, inv dec] 6 times. (18 sts)

Round 9: [1 sc, inv dec] 6 times. (12 sts)

Round 10: 1 sc in each st around.

Slst in next st, fasten off, cut yarn leaving a long tail for sewing. Folding the ear in half, sew along the top of the ear to close and create a pinched edge. Attach ears on each side of the donut hole, at the back of the icing, evenly spaced apart.

FINISHING TOUCHES

To add a flower to your sheep, make one in the colour of your choice (see **Accessories**), then sew securely to one ear.

Triceratops

This Donut Buddy may be from an older time, but she loves showing off her pretty frill and clean white horns to all her friends. See how proud she looks!

YOU WILL NEED

- Size 2.5mm (US B/1), 3mm (US C/2 or D/3) and 4mm (US G/6) hooks

- DK or worsted/Aran weight yarn in petrol, white, grass green and turquoise

- Donut making kit list (see **Basic Donut Pattern**)

- Safety eyes, 2 x 10-14mm*, or black yarn or black embroidery thread to make your own

*Safety eyes should **only** be used for children aged three years or older.*

DONUT

Follow the **Basic Donut Pattern** to create the donut base in petrol and the icing in grass green, omitting the sprinkles. If using safety eyes, place between rounds 4 and 5 of the icing.

FRILL BASE

Using 3mm hook and grass green, make 27 ch.

Row 1: starting in the 2nd ch from hook, 1 hdc in each st across, 1 ch (does not count as st here and throughout), turn. (26 sts)

Row 2: 2 hdc in the first st, 3 hdc, [2 hdc in the next st, 3 hdc] 5 times, 2 hdc, 1 ch, turn. (32 sts)

Row 3: 2 hdc in the first st, 3 hdc, [2 hdc in the next st, 3 hdc] 7 times, 1 ch, turn. (40 sts)

Row 4: 1 hdc in each st across, fasten off.

FRILL TOP

Using 3mm hook and turquoise, attach yarn to first st of Frill Base, 1 ch.

Row 1: 1 sc in first st, 5 dc in next st (shell st – see **Techniques**), [1 sc, 1 shell st] 18 times, 1 ch (does not count as st here and throughout), turn, leaving last 2 sts unworked. (19 shells sts)

Row 2: 1 sc, *5 dc in the sc between next 2 shell sts, sc in the top of the 3rd st of next shell st; rep from * to last shell st, 1 sc in the top of last sc. (18 shell sts)

Fasten off, cut yarn and weave in ends. Sew the frill at the back of the donut securely so that the top of the frill is above the donut slightly.

MOUTH

Using 3mm hook and grass green, make a magic ring.

Round 1: 6 sc into ring. (6 sts)

Round 2: 2 sc in each st around. (12 sts)

Round 3: [1 sc, 2 sc in next st] 6 times. (18 sts)

Round 4: 1 sc in each st around.

Round 5: [2 sc, 2 sc in next st] 6 times. (24 sts)

Round 6: Working in the blo (see **Crochet Techniques**), 1 sc in each st around.

Rounds 7 to 8: 1 sc in each st around.

Round 9: [2 sc, inv dec] 6 times. (18 sts)

Slst in next st, fasten off, cut yarn and leave a long tail for sewing. Lightly stuff and attach the mouth central to the donut ring hole.

LARGE HORNS (MAKE 2)

Using 2.5mm hook and white, make a magic ring.

Round 1: 4 sc into ring. (4 sts)

Round 2: [1 sc, 2 sc in next st] twice. (6 sts)

Round 3: [1 sc, 2 sc in next st] 3 times. (9 sts)

Rounds 4 to 6: 1 sc in each st around.

Slst in next st, fasten off, cut yarn and leave a long tail for sewing. Lightly stuff, then attach large horns, placing on either side of head and evenly spaced apart.

SMALL HORN

Using 2.5mm hook and white, make a magic ring.

Round 1: 4 sc into ring. (4 sts)

Round 2: [1 sc, 2 sc in next st] twice. (6 sts)

Rounds 3 to 4: 1 sc in each st around.

Slst in next st, fasten off, cut yarn and leave a long tail for sewing. Lightly stuff then attach horn at top of mouth in the centre.

EYES

If using safety eyes, these will already have been placed when making the donut. Alternatively, to make the toy suitable for children under three years of age, you can crochet or embroider the eyes (see **Basic Donut Pattern: Eyes**). Add a small fleck of white yarn to the outside edge of each eye with a darning needle. Sew either open or closed eyes just above the mouth if not using safety eyes.

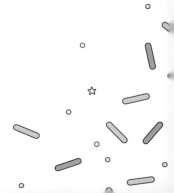

Duck

This energetic little duck loves nothing more than waddling and clucking along with her donut friends. Her cute head feathers make her an adorable sight.

YOU WILL NEED

- Size 3mm (US C/2 or D/3) and 4mm (US G/6) hooks
- DK or worsted/Aran weight yarn in parchment, citron and peach
- Embroidery thread in white
- Donut making kit list (see **Basic Donut Pattern**)
- Safety eyes, 2 x 10–14mm*, or black yarn or black embroidery thread to make your own

*Safety eyes should **only** be used for children aged three years or older.

DONUT

Follow the **Basic Donut Pattern** to create the donut base in parchment and the icing in citron, omitting the sprinkles. If using safety eyes, place between rounds 6 and 7 of the icing.

EYES

If using safety eyes, these will already have been placed when making the donut. Alternatively, to make the toy suitable for children under three years of age, you can crochet or embroider the eyes (see **Basic Donut Pattern: Eyes**). Using a darning needle and white embroidery thread, sew a white fleck of yarn around one half of each eye. Fasten off at the back and weave in ends.

HAIR

Using citron make 4 small hair tufts. Sew from the back of the icing to the front, making sure they are secured with a knot at the back. Trim to 1cm in length.

BEAK

Using 3mm hook and peach, make 9 ch.

Round 1: starting in the 2nd ch from hook, 7 sc, 2 sc in next st, working on the opposite side of the ch, 7 sc, 2 sc in next st. (18 sts)

Rounds 2 to 3: 1 sc in each st around.

Slst in next st, fasten off, cut yarn, leaving a long tail for sewing. Sew the beak 5 rows above the centre of the donut hole in a curved shape.

WINGS (MAKE 2)

Using 3mm hook and citron, make a magic ring.

Round 1: 4 sc into ring. (4 sts)

Round 2: 2 sc in each st around. (8 sts)

Round 3: [1 sc, 2 sc in next st] 4 times. (12 sts)

Rounds 4 to 5: 1 sc in each st around.

Round 6: [1 sc, 2 sc in next st] 6 times. (18 sts)

Round 7: 1 sc in each st around.

Round 8: [2 sc, 2 sc in next st] 6 times. (24 sts)

Rounds 9 to 12: 1 sc in each st around.

Round 13: [2 sc, inv dec] 6 times. (18 sts)

Round 14: [1 sc, inv dec] 6 times. (12 sts)

Round 15: [inv dec] 6 times.

Slst in next st, fasten off, cut yarn and close hole, leave a long tail for sewing. Sew the wings on either side of donut body, half over the icing and half over the base.

FEET (MAKE 2)

Using 3mm hook and peach, make a magic ring.

Round 1: 6 sc into ring. (6 sts)

Round 2: 2 sc in each st around. (12 sts)

Round 3: [1 sc, 2 sc in next st] 6 times. (18 sts)

Rounds 4 to 6: 1 sc in each st around.

Folding the feet in half, slst across to the other side sealing them shut, fasten off, cut yarn leaving a long tail for sewing. Sew to bottom of the donut.

Cow

With her lovely snout and different coloured ears, this cow is a sight to be seen. Add patches wherever you like and a flower in your choice of colour to complete her glamorous outfit.

YOU WILL NEED

- Size 3mm (US C/2 or D/3) and 4mm (US G/6) hooks

- DK or worsted/Aran weight yarn in parchment, white, apricot and black

- Donut making kit list (see **Basic Donut Pattern**)

- Safety eyes, 2 x 10–14mm*, or black yarn or black embroidery thread to make your own

*Safety eyes should **only** be used for children aged three years or older.

You can make your cow with as many spots as you like, or leave them off completely – make it your own!

DONUT

Follow the **Basic Donut Pattern** to create the donut base in parchment and the icing in white, omitting the sprinkles. If using safety eyes, place between rounds 4 and 5 of the icing.

EARS (MAKE 2: 1 WHITE, 1 BLACK)

Using 3mm hook and white or black, make a magic ring.

Round 1: 6 sc into ring. (6 sts)

Round 2: [2 sc, 2 sc in next st] twice. (8 sts)

Round 3: 1 sc in each st around.

Round 4: [1 sc, 2 sc in next st] 4 times. (12 sts)

Round 5: 1 sc in each st around.

Round 6: [1 sc, 2 sc in next st] 6 times. (18 sts)

Rounds 7 to 9: 1 sc in each st around.

Round 10: [inv dec] 9 times. (9 sts)

Slst in next st, fasten off, cut yarn leaving a long tail for sewing. Sew ears on each side of donut hole, at the back of the icing.

HORNS (MAKE 2)

Using 3mm hook and parchment, make a magic ring.

Round 1: 4 sc into ring. (4 sts)

Round 2: [1 sc, 2 sc in next st] twice. (6 sts)

Round 3: [1 sc, 2 sc in next st] 3 times. (9 sts)

Rounds 4 to 6: 1 sc in each st around.

Slst in next st, fasten off, cut yarn and leave a long tail for sewing. Lightly stuff then attach horns, placing on top of donut inside the gap between ears.

SNOUT

Using 3mm hook and apricot, make 9 ch.

Round 1: 2 sc in 2nd ch from the hook, 6 sc, 3 sc in last st, working around the foundation row, 6 sc, sc in the last st. (18 sts)

Round 2: 2 sc in first 2 sts, 6 sc, 2 sc in next 3 sts, 6 sc, 2 sc in next st. (24 sts)

Rounds 3 to 4: 1 sc in each st around.

Slst in next st, fasten off, cut yarn leaving a long tail for sewing. Lightly stuff and attach the snout central to donut ring hole.

Using a darning needle and dark pink yarn or embroidery thread, weave in two small nostrils evenly spaced apart. Fasten off at the back and weave in the ends.

EYES

If using safety eyes, these will already have been placed when making the donut. Alternatively, to make the toy suitable for children under three years of age, you can crochet or embroider the eyes (see **Basic Donut Pattern: Eyes**). Sew the eyes in the centre of donut above the Snout (if not using safety eyes).

COW PATCHES (MAKE 5)

Using 3mm hook and black, make 6 ch.

Round 1: sc in 2nd ch from hook and in each st across, 1 ch (does not count as a st throughout), turn. (5 sts)

Row 2: 1 sc, inv dec, 2 sc, 1 ch, turn. (4 sts)

Row 3: 1 sc, inv dec, 1 sc, 1 ch, turn. (3 sts)

Row 4: 1 sc, inv dec. (2 sts)

Fasten off, cut yarn, leaving a long tail for sewing. Attach cow patches to the donut wherever you like.

FINISHING TOUCHES

To add a flower to your cow, make one in a colour of your choice (see **Accessories**), then sew securely to bottom of one of the ears.

Fox

With his neat muzzle and button nose, this foxy buddy makes a handsome chap! He loves to strut around town, showing off his features. His donut friends think he is rather cool!

YOU WILL NEED

- Size 3mm (US C/2 or D/3) and 4mm (US G/6) hooks
- DK or worsted/Aran weight yarn in vintage peach, copper, cream and black
- Embroidery thread in white
- Donut making kit list (see **Basic Donut Pattern**)
- Safety eyes, 2 x 10–14mm*, or black yarn or black embroidery thread to make your own

*Safety eyes should **only** be used for children aged three years or older.*

To create a nice rounded nose, weave the black yarn back and forth, building up layers at the tip then around the base of the nose to finish it off.

DONUT

Follow the **Basic Donut Pattern** to create the donut base in vintage peach and the icing in copper, omitting the sprinkles. If using safety eyes, place between rounds 4 and 5 of the icing.

EARS (MAKE 2)

Using 4mm hook and black, make a magic ring.

Round 1: 6 sc into ring. (6 sts)

Round 2: [2 sc, 2 sc in next st] twice. (8 sts)

Round 3: 1 sc in each st around.

Change to copper.

Round 4: [1 sc, 2 sc in next st] 4 times. (12 sts)

Round 5: 1 sc in each st around.

Round 6: [1 sc, 2 sc in next st] 6 times. (18 sts)

Rounds 7 to 9: 1 sc in each st around.

Slst in next st, fasten off, cut yarn and leave a long tail for sewing. Sew ears on each side of donut hole, at the back of the icing, evenly spaced apart.

EYES

If using safety eyes, these will already have been placed when making the donut. Alternatively, to make the toy suitable for children under three years of age, you can crochet or embroider the eyes (see **Basic Donut Pattern: Eyes**). Using a darning needle and white embroidery thread, add a white line around one half of the eye.

MUZZLE

Using 4mm hook and cream, make a magic ring.

Round 1: 4 sc into ring. (4 sts)

Round 2: 2 sc in the first st, 2 sc, 2 sc in next st. (6 sts)

Round 3: 2 sc in the first 2 sts, 3 sc, 2 sc in next st. (9 sts)

Round 4: 3 sc, 2 sc in next st, 3 sc, 2 sc in the next 2 sts. (12 sts)

Round 5: 3 sc, 2 sc in next st, 5 sc, 2 sc in next st, 1 sc, 2 sc in next st. (15 sts)

Round 6: 2 sc in the first st, 3 sc, 2 sc in next st, 6 sc, 2 sc in next st, 3 sc. (18 sts)

Round 7: 2 sc in the first st, 4 sc, 2 sc in next st, 7 sc, 2 sc in next st, 4 sc. (21 sts)

Rounds 8 to 9: 1 sc in each st around.

Slst in next st, fasten off, cut yarn leaving a long tail for sewing. Lightly stuff and attach muzzle central to the donut ring hole.

MUZZLE PANEL

Using 3mm hook and copper, make 5 ch.

Row 1: starting in 2nd ch from hook, 1 sc in each st across, turn. (4 sts)

Row 2: 1 ch (does not count as a st throughout), 1 sc in each st across, turn.

Row 3: 1 ch, 2 sc in first st, 2 sc, 2 sc in next st, turn. (6 sts)

Row 4: 1 ch, 1 sc in each st across, turn.

Row 5: 1 ch, 2 sc in the first st, [1 sc, 2 sc in next st] twice, 1 sc, turn. (9 sts)

Rows 6 to 7: 1 ch, 1 sc in each st across.

Fasten off, cut yarn, leaving a long tail for sewing. Sew on top of muzzle.

Embroider a black nose at the tip by wrapping the yarn over and over in the same spot to create a bobble.

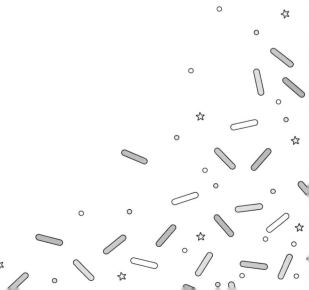

Teddy Bear

What a cuddly Donut Buddy this bear makes. Her multi-coloured nose and cute inner ears all add to the impression of a friendly little bear.

YOU WILL NEED

- Size 3mm (US C/2 or D/3) and 4mm (US G/6) hooks

- DK or worsted/Aran weight yarn in parchment, walnut and brown agate

- 4-ply cotton yarn in black

- Embroidery thread in white

- Donut making kit list (see **Basic Donut Pattern**)

- Safety eyes, 2 x 10–14mm*, or black yarn or black embroidery thread to make your own

*Safety eyes should **only** be used for children aged three years or older.*

You can use one colour yarn or use two strands of DK for the mouth and ear button to create a fun sprinkled effect.

DONUT

Follow the **Basic Donut Pattern** to create the donut base in parchment and the icing in walnut, omitting the sprinkles. If using safety eyes, place between rounds 4 and 5 of the icing.

EARS (MAKE 2)

Using 3mm hook and walnut, make a magic ring.

Round 1: 6 sc into ring. (6 sts)

Round 2: 2 sc in each st around. (12 sts)

Round 3: [1 sc, 2 sc in next st] 6 times. (18 sts)

Round 4: [5 sc, 2 sc in next st] 3 times. (21 sts)

Round 5: [5 sc, inv dec] 3 times. (18 sts)

Round 6: [4 sc, inv dec] 3 times. (15 sts)

Round 7: 1 sc in every st.

Slst in next st, fasten off, cut yarn and leave a long tail for sewing. Sew ears on each side of the donut hole, at the back of the icing, evenly spaced apart.

MIDDLE EARS (MAKE 2)

Using 4mm hook and brown agate, make a magic ring.

Round 1: 4 sc in magic ring, slst in next st, fasten off, cut yarn leaving a long tail for sewing.

Using a darning needle, sew the middle ears to the centre of each ear.

EYES

If using safety eyes, these will already have been placed when making the donut. Alternatively, to make the toy suitable for children under three years of age, you can crochet or embroider the eyes (see **Basic Donut Pattern: Eyes**). Using a darning needle and white embroidery thread, add a white line around one half of the eye. Sew on closed or open eyes in the centre of the donut above the muzzle if not using safety eyes.

MUZZLE

Using 3mm hook and brown agate, make a magic ring.

Round 1: 6 sc into ring. (6 sts)

Round 2: 2 sc in each st around. (12 sts)

Round 3: [1 sc, 2 sc in next st] 6 times. (18 sts)

Round 4: [2 sc, 2 sc in next st] 6 times. (24 sts)

Rounds 5 to 6: 1 sc in every st.

Slst in next st, fasten off, cut yarn, leaving a long tail for sewing. Embroider a nose and mouth in black cotton yarn onto the muzzle by weaving yarn back and forth until you get the desired effect. Lightly stuff and attach the muzzle central to the donut ring hole.

Giraffe

Safari playtime wouldn't be complete without a giraffe buddy! He loves to roam the hot plains in search of tasty leaves. His speckled ears and face add the cutest finishing touch.

YOU WILL NEED

- Size 3mm (US C/2 or D/3) and 4mm (US G/6) hooks

- DK or worsted/Aran weight yarn in mustard, walnut, brown agate, and parchment

- Embroidery thread in walnut and white

- Donut making kit list (see **Basic Donut Pattern**)

- Safety eyes, 2 x 10-14mm*, or black yarn or black embroidery thread to make your own

*Safety eyes should **only** be used for children aged three years or older.*

Add as many sprinkles to the giraffe's face as you would like or leave them off – make it your own! You can even change up the sprinkle colours!

DONUT

Follow the **Basic Donut Pattern** to create the donut base in parchment and the icing in mustard, omitting the sprinkles. If using safety eyes, place between rounds 4 and 5 of the icing.

EARS (MAKE 2)

Using 4mm hook and mustard, make a magic ring.

Round 1: 6 sc into ring. (6 sts)

Round 2: [2 sc, 2 sc in next st] twice. (8 sts)

Round 3: 1 sc in each st around.

Round 4: [1 sc, 2 sc in next st] 4 times. (12 sts)

Round 5: 1 sc in each st around.

Round 6: [1 sc, 2 sc in next st] 6 times. (18 sts)

Rounds 7 to 9: 1 sc in each st around.

Round 10: [inv dec] 9 times. (9 sts)

Slst in next st, fasten off, cut yarn and leave a long tail for sewing. Sew ears on each side of the donut hole, at the back of the icing, evenly spaced apart. Using a darning needle and walnut embroidery thread, weave in small sprinkle lines on both ears.

OSSICONES (MAKE 2)

Using 3mm hook and walnut, make a magic ring.

Round 1: 6 sc into ring. (6 sts)

Round 2: 2 sc in each st around. (12 sts)

Round 3: 1 sc in each st around.

Round 4: [inv dec] 6 times. (6 sts)

Rounds 5 to 6: 1 sc in each st around.

Slst in next st, fasten off, cut yarn and leave a long tail for sewing. Lightly stuff then attach the ossicones in the gap between the ears on the centre of the giraffe's head.

MUZZLE

Using 4mm hook and brown agate, make a magic ring.

Round 1: 6 sc into ring. (6 sts)

Round 2: 2 sc in each st around. (12 sts)

Round 3: [1 sc, 2 sc in next st] 6 times. (18 sts)

Round 4: [2 sc, 2 sc in next st] 6 times. (24 sts)

Round 5: [3 sc, 2 sc in next st] 6 times. (30 sts)

Rounds 6 to 8: 1 sc in each st around.

Slst in next st, fasten off, cut yarn leaving a long tail for sewing. Lightly stuff and attach the muzzle central to the donut ring hole, adding two nostril lines in walnut.

EYES

If using safety eyes, these will already have been placed when making the donut. Alternatively, to make the toy suitable for children under three years of age, you can crochet or embroider the eyes (see **Basic Donut Pattern: Eyes**). Using a darning needle and white embroidery thread, add a white line around one half of the eye. Sew on closed or open eyes in the centre of the donut above the muzzle if not using safety eyes.

Sunflower

Just sitting in the sun brings the best out of this bright and beautiful Donut Buddy. She loves to attract the bees and grows tall and proud among the wildflowers.

YOU WILL NEED

- Size 2.5mm (US B/1) and 4mm (US G/6) hooks

- DK or worsted/Aran weight yarn in mocha, daffodil yellow, shrimp, white or cream and black

- Embroidery thread in white

- Donut making kit list (see **Basic Donut Pattern**)

- Safety eyes, 2 x 10–14mm*, or black yarn or black embroidery thread to make your own

*Safety eyes should **only** be used for children aged three years or older.*

DONUT

Follow the **Basic Donut Pattern** to create the donut base and the icing in mocha. If using safety eyes, place between rounds 4 and 5 of the icing.

PETALS (MAKE 10)

Using 2.5mm hook and daffodil yellow, make a magic ring.

Round 1: 6 sc into ring. (6 sts)

Round 2: 2 sc in each st around. (12 sts)

Round 3: [1 sc, 2sc in next st] 6 times. (18 sts)

Rounds 4 to 8: 1 sc in each st around.

Round 9: [1 sc, inv dec] 6 times. (12 sts)

Rounds 10 to 11: 1 sc in each st around.

Slst in next st, fasten off, cut yarn leaving a long tail for sewing.

EYES

If using safety eyes, these will already have been placed when making the donut. Alternatively, to make the toy suitable for children under three years of age, you can crochet or embroider the eyes (see **Basic Donut Pattern: Eyes**). Using a darning needle and white embroidery thread, add a white line around one half of the eye. Sew on closed or open eyes in the centre of the donut below the donut ring hole if not using safety eyes.

MOUTH

Sew on a small smile in a V-shape just below the eyes in shrimp.

BUMBLE BEE APPLIQUÉ

Body

Using 2.5mm hook and daffodil yellow, make a magic ring.

Round 1: 6 sc into ring. (6 sts)

Round 2: 1 ch, 2 sc in next 2 sts, 2 hdc in next 2 sts, 2 dc in next st, 2 hdc in next st. (12 sts)

Round 3: 2 sc in the next 3 sts, 1 hdc, 5 sc, slst in next st.

Fasten off, cut yarn, leaving a long tail for sewing.

Wings

Using 2.5mm hook and join white or cream to top of one of the sc, 5 ch, slst in next st, 5 ch, slst back in the same st, fasten off, cut yarn and weave in ends.

Stripes

Using black yarn, weave vertical lines from back to front, evenly spaced apart, fasten off at the back and weave in ends. Sew appliqué to one petal and fasten off securely at the back.

Sew the petals to donut base without stuffing, evenly spaced apart.

Crab

This little fella crawls sideways along the sandy shores. He finds morsels to eat with his pincers and is always happy to have a pretty starfish resting on his shell.

YOU WILL NEED

- Size 3mm (US C/2 or D/3) and 4mm (US G/6) hooks
- DK or worsted/Aran weight yarn in apricot and shrimp
- Donut making kit list (see **Basic Donut Pattern**)
- Safety eyes, 2 x 10–14mm*, or black yarn or black embroidery thread to make your own

*Safety eyes should **only** be used for children aged three years or older.*

DONUT

Follow the **Basic Donut Pattern** to create the donut base in apricot and the icing in shrimp, omitting the sprinkles. If using safety eyes, place between rounds 6 and 7 of the icing.

PINCERS (MAKE 4)

Using 3mm hook and shrimp, make a magic ring.

Round 1: 4 sc into ring. (4 sts)

Round 2: 2 sc in each st around. (8 sts)

Round 3: [1 sc, 2 sc in next st] 4 times. (12 sts)

Rounds 4 to 6: 1 sc in each st around.

Slst in next st, fasten off (on 2 of the 4 pieces only). Cut the yarn, leaving a long tail for sewing.

Round 7: Holding 2 parts together, 1 sc in both loops of 1 st from each section to connect them, 1 sc in the same st, 1 sc in each st around. (24 sts)

Round 8: 1 sc in each st around.

Round 9: [1 sc, inv dec] 8 times. (16 sts)

Round 10: [inv dec] 8 times. (8 sts)

Rounds 11 to 12: 1 sc in each st around.

Slst in next st, fasten off, cut yarn leaving a long tail for sewing. Lightly stuff pincers and attach at front of donut halfway between the icing and donut base.

EYES

If using safety eyes, these will already have been placed when making the donut. Alternatively, to make the toy suitable for children under three years of age, you can crochet or embroider the eyes (see **Basic Donut Pattern: Eyes**). Sew on eyes in the centre of the donut below the donut ring hole if not using safety eyes.

MOUTH

Sew on a small smile in a V-shape just below the eyes using black embroidery thread.

LEGS (MAKE 6)

Using 3mm hook and apricot, make a magic ring.

Round 1: 4 sc into ring. (4 sts)

Rounds 2 to 6: 1 sc in each st around.

Slst in next st, fasten off, cut yarn leaving a long tail for sewing. Sew 3 legs on either side of donut, evenly spaced apart.

FINISHING TOUCHES

To add a starfish to your crab, make one in cobalt blue (see **Accessories**), then sew securely at the back of the crab's body.

Sew each leg one after the other leaving a small gap between each one.

Jellyfish

Propelling himself along with his wonderful multi-coloured tentacles and frill, this jellyfish has a lovely time when in the water. Don't worry – he's not the stinging kind!

YOU WILL NEED

- Size 3mm (US C/2 or D/3) and 4mm (US G/6) hooks

- DK or worsted/Aran weight yarn in apricot, green, turquoise, pink, bluebell, yellow and orange

- Donut making kit list (see **Basic Donut Pattern**)

- Safety eyes, 2 x 10–14mm*, or black yarn or black embroidery thread to make your own

*Safety eyes should **only** be used for children aged three years or older.*

DONUT BASE

Follow the **Basic Donut Pattern** to create the donut base only in orange.

ICING

Using 4mm hook and apricot, make 20 ch, join to make a circle (20 sts).

Round 1: 1 ch (does not count as st), 1 sc in same st, 2 sc in next st, [1 sc, 2sc in next st] 9 times. (30 sts)

Round 2: 1 sc in each st around.

Round 3: [2 sc, 2 sc in next st] 10 times. (40 sts)

Round 4: 1 sc in each st around.

Round 5: [3 sc, 2 sc in next st] 10 times. (50 sts)

Rounds 6 to 8: 1 sc in each st around.

Round 9: inv dec, 48 sc. (49 sts)

Round 10: 1 ch, 5 dc in first st, *skip next st, slst in next st, 5 hdc in next st, skip next st, slst in next st, 5 dc in next st; rep from * to the end of round, slst in the first ch-sp.

Fasten off, leaving a long tail for sewing. If using safety eyes, place between rounds 4 and 5 of the icing.

Sew icing onto the donut starting from the small hole in the centre, then sew the edges of the icing to the donut, being careful not to sew down the icing drips.

LONG CURLED TENTACLES (MAKE 4: 1 EACH IN GREEN, YELLOW, PINK & ORANGE)

Using 3mm hook make 50 ch.

Row 1: 3 sc in 2nd ch from hook and each st across. (147 sts)

Fasten off, cut yarn, leaving a long tail for sewing.

SHORT CURLED TENTACLES (MAKE 2; 1 EACH IN TURQUOISE & BLUEBELL)

Using 3mm hook make 30 ch.

Row 1: 3 sc in 2nd ch from hook and each st across. (87 sts)

Fasten off, cut yarn, leaving a long tail for sewing.

LONG STRAIGHT TENTACLES (MAKE 6: 1 EACH IN COLOURS OF CURLED TENTACLES)

Using 3mm hook make 35 ch.

Row 1: 1 sc in 2nd ch from hook and each st across. (34 sts)

Fasten off and cut yarn, leaving a long tail for sewing.

EYES

If using safety eyes, these will already have been placed when making the donut. Alternatively, to make the toy suitable for children under three years of age, you can crochet or embroider the eyes (see **Basic Donut Pattern: Eyes**). If embroidering eyes, use yarn or embroidery thread and make little upside-down V-shapes, evenly spaced apart, 4 sts wide to give a cute look.

MOUTH

Sew on a small smile in a V-shape just below the eyes using apricot.

CHEEKS (MAKE 2)

Use a 3mm hook and pink yarn.

Round 1: 5 sc into a magic ring, slst in next st, fasten off, cut yarn, leaving a long tail for sewing. (5 sts)

Attach the cheeks just below and to the side of the eyes.

FINISHING TOUCHES

Make a starfish in melon pink (see **Accessories**). Sew to the front.

Unicorn

This adorable unicorn is a great friend to all her Donut Buddies. She's very proud of her colourful horn, sprinkled ears and flowing mane, and she loves shaking her head to make it swirl.

YOU WILL NEED

- Size 3mm (US C/2 or D/3) and 4mm (US G/6) hooks

- DK or worsted/Aran weight yarn in white, grey, lemon, sage, shrimp, bright pink and lavender

- Embroidery thread in various colours

- Donut making kit list (see **Basic Donut Pattern**)

- Safety eyes, 2 x 10–14mm*, or black yarn or black embroidery thread to make your own

*Safety eyes should **only** be used for children aged three years or older.*

You can make your unicorn horn in one block colour or like mine make it rainbow for a vibrant look.

DONUT

Follow the **Basic Donut Pattern** to create the donut base and the icing in white, omitting the sprinkles. If using safety eyes, place between rounds 4 and 5 of the icing.

EARS (MAKE 2)

Using 3mm hook and white, make a magic ring.

Round 1: 6 sc into ring. (6 sts)

Round 2: [2 sc, 2 sc in next st] twice. (8 sts)

Round 3: 1 sc in each st around.

Round 4: [1 sc, 2 sc in next st] 4 times. (12 sts)

Round 5: 1 sc in each st around.

Round 6: [1 sc, 2 sc in next st] 6 times. (18 sts)

Rounds 7 to 9: 1 sc in each st around.

Round 10: [inv dec] 9 times. (9 sts)

Slst in next st, fasten off, cut yarn and leave a long tail for sewing. Sew ears on each side of the donut hole, at the back of the icing, evenly spaced apart. Using a darning needle and embroidery thread, add sprinkles to each ear in as many colours as you wish.

EYES

If using safety eyes, these will already have been placed when making the donut. Alternatively, to make the toy suitable for children under three years of age, you can crochet or embroider the eyes (see **Basic Donut Pattern: Eyes**). Using black embroidery thread and a darning needle, sew a small line around the top of each eye to create a hooded eye effect. Sew on closed eyes if not using safety eyes, just above the muzzle.

HORN

Using 3mm hook and lavender, make 12 ch. Join with a slst making sure not to twist your work, 1 ch.

Rounds 1 to 2: 1 sc in each st around.

Change to bright pink.

Round 3: [4 sc, inv dec] twice. (10 sts)

Round 4: 1 sc in each st around.

Change to shrimp.

Round 5: [3 sc, inv dec] twice. (8 sts)

Round 6: 1 sc in each st around.

Change to sage.

Round 7: [2 sc, inv dec] twice. (6 sts)

Round 8: 1 sc in each st around.

Change to lemon.

Round 9: [Inv dec] 3 times. (3 sts)

Slst in next st, fasten off, cut yarn and weave in ends. Lightly stuff and attach the horn, placing in centre of top of donut.

MUZZLE

Using 4mm hook and grey, make a magic ring.

Round 1: 6 sc into ring. (6 sts)

Round 2: [3 sc in the first st, 2 sc in next st, 1 sc] twice. (12 sts)

Round 3: 1 sc, 2 sc in the next 3 sts, 3 sc, 2 sc in the next 3 sts, 2 sc. (18 sts)

Round 4: 2 sc, [2 sc in next st, 1 sc] twice, 2 sc in next st, 4 sc, [2 sc in next st, 1 sc], twice, 2 sc in next st, 2 sc. (24 sts)

Rounds 5 to 6: 1 sc in each st, around.

Slst in next st, then fasten off. Cut yarn, leaving a long tail for sewing. Lightly stuff and attach muzzle central to the donut ring hole.

HAIR

Attach strands of coloured yarn to bottom of horn to create a long mane.

See **Crochet Techniques: Attaching the Hair** to see the basic technique for attaching the hair.

Red Panda

Striking ears, cheeks and eyebrows make this panda Donut Buddy stand out in the crowd. Practice your embroidery skills to complete his features and make him a happy boy.

YOU WILL NEED

- Size 2.5mm (US B/1) and 4mm (US G/6) hooks

- DK or worsted/Aran weight yarn in copper, cream, black and white (optional)

- Embroidery thread in white

- Donut making kit list (see **Basic Donut Pattern**)

- Safety eyes, 2 x 10–14mm*, or black yarn or black embroidery thread to make your own

*Safety eyes should **only** be used for children aged three years or older.*

DONUT

Follow the **Basic Donut Pattern** to create the donut base and the icing in copper, omitting the sprinkles. If using safety eyes, place them between rounds 4 and 5 of the icing.

MUZZLE

Using 2.5mm hook and cream or white, make a magic ring.

Round 1: 6 sc into ring. (6 sts)

Round 2: 2 sc in each st around. (12 sts)

Round 3: [1 sc, 2 sc in next st] 6 times. (18 sts)

Round 4: 5 sc, 3 sc in next st, 7 sc, 3 sc in next st, 4 sc. (22 sts)

Rounds 5 to 6: 1 sc in each st around.

Slst in next st, fasten off, cut yarn leaving a long tail for sewing. Lightly stuff, then attach muzzle in line with donut hole. Embroider a nose onto mouth using a darning needle and black yarn (6 sts wide by 3 sts in length) and a small mouth line.

EARS (MAKE 2)

Inner

Using 2.5mm hook and black, make 4 ch.

Row 1: Slst in 2nd ch from hook, 1 hdc, 1 dc.

Fasten off, cut yarn leaving a long tail for sewing.

Outer

Using 2.5mm hook and cream, make a magic ring.

Round 1: 6 sc into ring. (6 sts)

Round 2: [2 sc, 2 sc in next st] twice. (8 sts)

Round 3: 1 sc in each st around.

Round 4: [1 sc, 2 sc in next st] 4 times. (12 sts)

Round 5: 1 sc in each st around.

Round 6: [1 sc, 2 sc in next st] 6 times. (18 sts)

Round 7: 1 sc in each st around.

Slst in next st, fasten off, cut yarn, leaving a long tail for sewing. Using a darning needle and copper, weave small lines around the edges of the ear [A], adding more at the tip of the ear then back down the other side [B], fasten off at the base leaving a long tail for sewing. Sew inner black triangle to the ear and attach ears to side of donut (do not stuff), evenly spaced apart.

EYES

If using safety eyes, these will already have been placed when making the donut. Alternatively, to make the toy suitable for children under three years of age, you can crochet or embroider the eyes (see **Basic Donut Pattern: Eyes**).

EYEBROWS (MAKE 2)

Using a darning needle and cream or white, weave small lines 1 st wide by 1 st long from the front to the back of the icing roughly 1cm above the eye, fasten off securely at the back.

CHEEKS (MAKE 2)

Using a darning needle and cream or white, weave small lines level with the eyebrow, down to the start of the mouth from the front to the back of the icing, 2 sts wide and approximately 5cm in length, fasten off securely at the back.

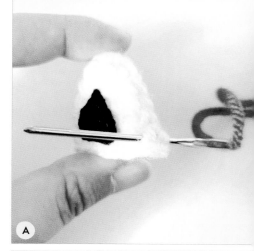

Snowman

Brrrr! This snowman needs his scarf and mittens to keep the chill out. Decorate him with a fabulous top hat and carrot nose to complete his winter ensemble.

YOU WILL NEED

- Size 2.5mm (US B/1) and 3mm (US C/2 or D/3) hooks

- DK or worsted/Aran weight yarn in white, dark red, black and orange

- Embroidery thread in white

- Donut making kit list (see **Basic Donut Pattern**)

- Safety eyes, 2 x 10–14mm*, or black yarn or black embroidery thread to make your own

*Safety eyes should **only** be used for children aged three years or older.*

DONUT

Follow the **Basic Donut Pattern** to create the donut base and the icing in white, omitting the sprinkles.

HEAD

Using 3mm hook and white, make a magic ring.

Round 1: 6 sc into ring. (6 sts)

Round 2: 2 sc in each st around. (12 sts)

Round 3: [1 sc, 2 sc in next st] 6 times. (18 sts)

Round 4: [2 sc, 2 sc in next st] 6 times. (24 sts)

Round 5: [3 sc, 2 sc in next st] 6 times. (30 sts)

Round 6: [4 sc, 2 sc in next st] 6 times. (36 sts)

Place safety eyes between rounds 9 and 10.

Rounds 7 to 12: 1 sc in each st around.

Round 13: [4 sc, inv dec] 6 times. (30 sts)

Round 14: [3 sc, inv dec] 6 times. (24 sts)

Stuff head firmly.

Round 15: [2 sc, inv dec] 6 times. (18 sts)

Add a little more stuffing.

Round 16: [1 sc, inv dec] 6 times. (12 sts)

Round 17: [Inv dec] 6 times. (6 sts)

Slst in next st, fasten off, cut yarn, leaving a long tail for sewing. Stuff firmly then attach at the top of the donut body.

EYES

If using safety eyes, these will already have been placed when making the head. Alternatively, to make the toy suitable for children under three years of age, you can crochet or embroider the eyes (see **Basic Donut Pattern: Eyes**).

NOSE

Using 3mm hook and orange, make a magic ring.

Round 1: 4 sc into ring. (4 sts)

Round 2: 2 sc in the first st, 3 sc. (5 sts)

Round 3: 2 sc in the first st, 4 sc. (6 sts)

Round 4: 2 sc in the first st, 5 sc. (7 sts)

Round 5: 2 sc in the first st, 6 sc. (8 sts)

Slst in next st, fasten off, cut yarn leaving a long tail for sewing. Lightly stuff and sew nose just below eyes.

SCARF

Using 3mm hook and dark red, make 45 ch.

Row 1: 1 sc in 2nd ch from hook and each st across, 1 ch (does not count as a st), turn. (44 sts)

Row 2: 1 hdc in each st across.

Fasten off, cut yarn and weave in ends. Using a darning needle, thread strands of dark red yarn at scarf ends to make tassels, making sure to tie ends tightly. Sew scarf around neck and onto body.

HAT

Using 3mm hook and black, make a magic ring.

Round 1: 10 sc into ring. (10 sts)

Round 2: 1 sc into the first st, 2 sc into the next st; repeat all the way around. (15 sts)

Round 3: 1 sc into the first 2 sts, 2 sc into the next st; repeat all the way around. (20 sts)

Round 4: 1 sc into the first 4 sts, 2 sc into the next st; repeat all the way around. (24 sts)

Round 5: working in blo; (see **Crochet Techniques**): 1 sc into each st all the way around. (24 sts)

Round 6: working back into both loops; 1 sc into the first 4 sts, inv dec into the next st; repeat all the way around. (20 sts)

Round 7: 1 sc into the first 2 sts, inv dec into the next st; repeat all the way around. (15 sts)

Rounds 8 to 9: 1 sc in each st around (2 rounds). (15 sts)

Round 10: working into the flo; 1 sc into each st around. (15 sts)

Round 11: working back into both loops; 2 sc into each st around, slst, fasten off, cut yarn, leaving a long tail for sewing. (30 sts)

Lightly stuff and sew hat on top of head.

HAT TRIM

Using 2.5mm hook and dark red, ch as many stitches as you need to attach all the way around brim of hat, Sew onto hat using a darning needle, fasten off, cut yarn. Weave in ends.

HAT SNOWFLAKE

Using a darning needle and white embroidery thread, sew a small snowflake in centre of hat. Fasten off securely inside hat.

BUTTON

Using 2.5mm hook and black, make a magic ring.

Round 1: 4 sc in ring. (4 sts).

Slst in next st, fasten off, cut yarn, leaving a long tail for sewing. Sew in centre of donut body. For older children you can use a button or a flat back resin and sew or glue securely to donut.

MITTENS & ARMS (MAKE 2)

Using 3mm hook and dark red, make a magic ring.

Round 1: 6 sc into ring. (6 sts)

Round 2: 2 sc in each st around. (12 sts)

Rounds 3 to 4: 1 sc in each st around.

Round 5: 5 sc, BS (bobble) in next st (see **Crochet Techniques**), 6 sc.

Round 6: [2 sc, inv dec] 3 times. (9 sts)

Round 7: Working in Flo: 2 sc in each st around, fasten off, cut yarn and weave in ends. (18 sts)

Change to white.

Round 8: Working in blo of round 6: 1 sc in each st around. (9 sts)

Rounds 9 to 14: 1 sc in every st.

Slst in next st, fasten off, cut yarn, leaving a long tail for sewing. Lightly stuff arms and mittens and attach either side of the donut body.

Dog

Jumping around and shaking his floppy ears to his heart's content is this sweet dog's favourite pastime! He also loves to show off his shiny new collar and tag to all his Donut Buddy pals.

YOU WILL NEED

- Size 2.5mm (US B/1), 3mm (US C/2 or D/3) and 4mm (US G/6) hooks

- DK or worsted/Aran weight yarn in walnut and parchment

- 4-ply cotton yarn in red and mustard

- Embroidery thread in white

- Donut making kit list (see **Basic Donut Pattern**)

- Safety eyes, 2 x 10–14mm*, or black yarn or black embroidery thread to make your own

*Safety eyes should **only** be used for children aged three years or older.

Sew the tag to the collar, then stitch the collar to the base of the donut so it sits nicely on your sweet little pup!

DONUT

Follow the **Basic Donut Pattern** to create the donut base in walnut and the icing in parchment, omitting the sprinkles. If using safety eyes, place between rounds 4 and 5 of the icing.

EARS (MAKE 2)

Using 3mm hook and walnut, make a magic ring.

Round 1: 8 sc into ring. (8 sts)

Round 2: 2 sc in each st around. (16 sts)

Rounds 3 to 4: 1 sc in each st around.

Round 5: [1 sc, 2 sc in next st] 8 times. (24 sts)

Rounds 6 to 7: 1 sc in each st around.

Round 8: [2 sc, 2 sc in next st] 8 times. (32 sts)

Rounds 9 to 11: 1 sc in each st around.

Round 12: [2 sc, inv dec] 8 times. (24 sts)

Round 13: 1 sc in each st around.

Round 14: [2 sc, inv dec] 6 times. (18 sts)

Round 15: 1 sc in each st around.

Round 16: [1 sc, inv dec] 6 times. (12 sts)

Rounds 17 to 19: 1 sc in each st around.

Slst in next st, fasten off, cut yarn leaving a long tail for sewing. Sew ears on each side of donut hole, at the back of the icing. (A squeaker or rattle can also be placed inside the ear if desired).

EYES

If using safety eyes, these will already have been placed when making the donut. Alternatively, to make the toy suitable for children under three years of age, you can crochet or embroider the eyes (see **Basic Donut Pattern: Eyes**). Using a darning needle and white embroidery thread, add a white line around one half of the eye.

MUZZLE

Using 3mm hook and parchment, make a magic ring.

Round 1: 6 sc into ring. (6 sts)

Round 2: 2 sc in each st around. (12 sts)

Round 3: [1 sc, 2 sc in next st] 6 times. (18 sts)

Round 4: [2 sc, 2 sc in the next 3 sts, 4 sc] twice. (24 sts)

Rounds 5 to 6: 1 sc in each st around.

Round 7: [2 sc, inv dec] 6 times. (18 sts)

Slst in next st, fasten off, cut yarn, leaving a long tail for sewing. Lightly stuff and attach to the icing, central to the donut ring hole. Embroider a nose and mouth onto muzzle using walnut by weaving yarn back and forth for desired effect.

COLLAR

Using 2.5mm hook and red, make 6 ch.

Row 1: starting in the 2nd ch from hook, 5 sc, turn. (5 sts)

Rows 2 to 16: 1 ch (does not count as st throughout), 1 sc in each st across, turn.

Fasten off, cut yarn, leaving a long tail for sewing.

COLLAR TAG

Using 2.5mm hook and mustard, make a magic ring.

Round 1: 6 sc into ring. (6 sts)

Round 2: 2 sc in each st around. (12 sts)

Round 3: [1 sc, 2 sc in next st] 6 times. (18 sts)

Slst in next st, fasten off, cut yarn, leaving a long tail for sewing. Sew the tag to the collar, then sew the collar between the icing and the donut, just below the muzzle.

Snail

You can make this pretty snail in two sizes using the same basic pattern with a different size hook and thickness of yarn. Add some flowers to her shell for a pretty finishing touch!

YOU WILL NEED

- Size 3mm (US C/2 or D/3) and 4mm (US G/6) hooks

- DK or worsted/Aran weight yarn in rust, peach and pomegranate

- Embroidery thread in pink

- Donut making kit list (see **Basic Donut Pattern**)

- Safety eyes, 2 x 10–14mm*, or black yarn or black embroidery thread to make your own

*Safety eyes should **only** be used for children aged three years or older.

You can add as many flowers as you want here or leave them off completely, or why not add a bow tie for a sophisticated look!

DONUT

Follow the **Basic Donut Pattern** to create the donut base in rust, the icing in pomegranate and the sprinkles in peach.

HEAD & BODY

Using 4mm hook and peach, make a magic ring.

Round 1: 6 sc into ring. (6 sts)

Round 2: 2 sc in each st around. (12 sts)

Round 3: [1 sc, 2 sc in next st] 6 times. (18 sts)

Round 4: [2 sc, 2 sc in next st] 6 times. (24 sts)

Round 5: [3 sc, 2 sc in next st] 6 times. (30 sts)

Round 6: [4 sc, 2 sc in next st] 6 times. (36 sts)

Rounds 7 to 12: 1 sc in each st around.

If using safety eyes, place them between rounds 8 and 9 of the head.

Round 13: [10 sc, inv dec] 3 times. (33 sts)

Round 14: [9 dc, inv dec] 3 times. (30 sts)

Round 15: [8 sc, inv dec] 3 times. (27 sts)

Round 16: [7 dc, inv dec] 3 times. (24 sts)

Round 17: [6 sc, inv dec] 3 times. (21 sts)

Round 18: [5 sc, inv dec] 3 times. (18 sts)

Stuff the head firmly, the rest of the body will not be stuffed.

Round 19: [4 sc, inv dec] 3 times. (15 sts)

Rounds 20 to 35: 1 sc in each st around.

Round 36: [3 sc, inv dec] 3 times. (12 sts)

Round 37: 1 sc in each st around.

Round 38: [2 sc, inv dec] 3 times. (9 sts)

Round 39: 1 sc in each st around.

Round 40: [1 sc, inv dec] 3 times. (6 sts)

Slst in next st, fasten off, cut yarn and sew hole closed. Attach body to base of donut and along one side by weaving the yarn in and out to secure tightly.

EYES

If using safety eyes, these will already have been placed when making the head. Alternatively, to make the toy suitable for children under three years of age, you can crochet or embroider the eyes (see **Basic Donut Pattern: Eyes**).

MOUTH

Using a darning needle and pink embroidery thread, sew a small smile just below the eyes by creating a "V" shape. Add small horizontal lines for cheeks if desired. Fasten off, cut yarn and weave in ends.

FEELERS (MAKE 2)

Using 3mm hook and pomegranate, make a magic ring.

Round 1: 4 sc into ring. (4 sts)

Rounds 2 to 4: 1 sc in each st around.

Slst in next st, fasten off, cut yarn, leaving a long tail for sewing. Sew feelers on top of head, evenly spaced apart.

FINISHING TOUCHES

To add flowers to your snail, make one each in 4-ply cotton yarn in lime, lemonade, pale peach and lavender (see **Accessories**), then sew securely to the icing.

If you would like to make your snail in plush yarn use this pattern and a 4.5mm hook with Himalaya Dolphine baby yarn by Hobium Yarns or any plush yarn you choose.

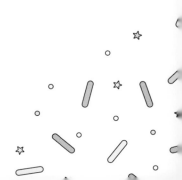

Reindeer

With his cute red nose and strong antlers, this reindeer is ready to take to the sky pulling a sleigh full of toys. Make a wish to help him fly as high as can be!

YOU WILL NEED

- Size 3mm (US C/2 or D/3) and 4mm (US G/6) hooks

- DK or worsted/Aran weight yarn in buttermilk, beige, walnut and red

- Donut making kit list (see **Basic Donut Pattern**)

- Safety eyes, 2 x 10–14mm*, or black yarn or black embroidery thread to make your own

*Safety eyes should **only** be used for children aged three years or older.*

Crochet a red or black nose, the choice is yours! Create a Dasher, Dancer, Prancer or Vixen instead!

DONUT

Follow the **Basic Donut Pattern** to create the donut base in buttermilk and the icing in beige, omitting the sprinkles. If using safety eyes, place between rounds 4 and 5 of the icing.

EARS (MAKE 2)

Using 4mm hook and beige, make a magic ring.

Round 1: 5 sc into ring. (5 sts)

Round 2: 2 sc in each st around. (10 sts)

Round 3: [1 sc, 2 sc in next st] 5 times. (15 sts)

Rounds 4 to 6: 1 sc in each st around.

Slst in next st, fasten off, cut yarn, leaving a long tail for sewing. Sew ears on each side of donut hole, at the back of the icing.

EYES

If using safety eyes, these will already have been placed when making the icing. Alternatively, to make the toy suitable for children under three years of age, you can crochet or embroider the eyes (see **Basic Donut Pattern: Eyes**).

MUZZLE

Using 4mm hook and beige, make a magic ring.

Round 1: 6 sc into ring. (6 sts)

Round 2: 2 sc in each st around. (12 sts)

Round 3: [1 sc, 2 sc in next st] 6 times. (18 sts)

Round 4: [2 sc, 2 sc in next st] 6 times. (24 sts)

Round 5: [3 sc, 2 sc in next st] 6 times. (30 sts)

Rounds 6 to 7: 1 sc in each st around.

Slst in next st, fasten off, cut yarn, leaving a long tail for sewing.

NOSE

Using 3mm hook and red, make a magic ring.

Round 1: 6 sc into ring. (6 sts)

Round 2: 2 sc in each st around. (12 sts)

Rounds 3 to 4: 1 sc in each st around.

Slst in next st, fasten off, cut yarn, leaving a long tail for sewing. Attach nose, placing it in the centre of muzzle, lightly stuff and sew muzzle onto icing making sure nose is in line with donut hole.

LARGE ANTLERS (MAKE 2)

Using 3mm hook and walnut, make a magic ring.

Round 1: 8 sc into ring. (8 sts)

Rounds 2 to 12: 1 sc in each st around.

Slst in next st, fasten off, cut yarn, leaving a long tail for sewing.

MEDIUM ANTLERS (MAKE 2)

Using 3mm hook and walnut, make a magic ring.

Round 1: 6 sc into ring. (6 sts)

Rounds 2 to 4: 1 sc in each st around.

Slst in next st, fasten off, cut yarn leaving a long tail for sewing.

SMALL ANTLERS (MAKE 2)

Using 3mm hook and walnut, make a magic ring.

Round 1: 4 sc into ring. (4 sts)

Rounds 2 to 3: 1 sc in each st around.

Slst in next st, fasten off, cut yarn, leaving a long tail for sewing. Lightly stuff and sew the antlers together with one medium and one small antler attached to each side of one long antler, then attach either side of the ears.

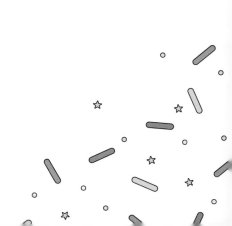

Cat

This happy little cat has a cute pink nose and adorable inner ears. She loves to play outdoors with her Donut Buddies! Add a sweet collar and tag for the purrrfect finishing touches.

YOU WILL NEED

- Size 3mm (US C/2 or D/3) and 4mm (US G/6) hooks
- DK or worsted/Aran weight yarn in cream and grey
- 4-ply cotton yarn in bright pink, peach and lavender
- Embroidery thread in pink and blue
- Donut making kit list (see **Basic Donut Pattern**)
- Safety eyes, 2 x 10–14mm*, or black yarn or black embroidery thread to make your own

*Safety eyes should **only** be used for children aged three years or older.

You can add whiskers to your cat by sewing three strands of yarn to each side of the mouth, or, like mine, leave them off. The choice is yours!

DONUT

Follow the **Basic Donut Pattern** to create the donut base in cream and the icing in grey, omitting the sprinkles. If using safety eyes, place between rounds 4 and 5 of the icing.

EARS (MAKE 2)

Using 3mm hook and grey, make a magic ring.

Round 1: 6 sc into ring. (6 sts)

Round 2: 1 sc in each st around.

Round 3: 2 sc in each st around. (12 sts)

Round 4: 1 sc in each st around.

Round 5: [1 sc, 2 sc in next st] 6 times. (18 sts)

Round 6: 1 sc in each st around.

Round 7: [2 sc, 2 sc in next st] 6 times. (24 sts)

Rounds 8 to 9: 1 sc in each st around.

Round 10: [2 sc, inv dec] 6 times. (18 sts)

Slst in next st, fasten off, cut yarn leaving a long tail for sewing.

INSIDE EARS (MAKE 2)

Using 3mm hook and bright pink, make a magic ring.

Round 1: 6 sc into ring. (6 sts)

Slst in next st, fasten off, cut yarn leaving a long tail for sewing. Sew inside part of ear to main ear. Attach ears to the donut, evenly spaced apart, at the back of the icing.

MUZZLE

Using 4mm hook and cream, make a magic ring.

Round 1: 6 sc into ring. (6 sts)

Round 2: 2 sc in each st around. (12 sts)

Round 3: [1 sc, 2 sc in next st] 6 times. (18 sts)

Round 4: 2 sc, 2 sc in next 3 sts, 6 sc, 2 sc in next 3 sts, 4 sc. (24 sts)

Rounds 5 to 6: 1 sc in each st around.

Round 7: 2 sc, inv dec into the next st; repeat all the way around. (18 sts)

Slst in next st, fasten off, cut yarn leaving a long tail for sewing.

NOSE

Using pink embroidery thread, sew a nose in a V-shape, then fill in the gaps by continuously weaving the yarn through until you are happy with the shape. Add a mouth line 2 stitches long that is central to the nose.

WHISKERS (MAKE 6)

Cut strands of yarn or embroidery thread to the desired length in colour of your choice, and weave 3 whiskers each side of the nose from the back to the front.

Lightly stuff the muzzle and attach central to the donut ring hole.

EYES

If using safety eyes, these will already have been placed when making the head. Alternatively, to make the toy suitable for children under three years of age, you can crochet or embroider the eyes (see **Basic Donut Pattern: Eyes**). Using a darning needle and blue embroidery thread, add a fleck of yarn around the top half of the eye. Fasten off at the back and weave in ends.

COLLAR

Using 3mm hook and peach, make 4 ch.

Row 1: starting in the 2nd ch from hook, 3 sc, turn. (3 sts)

Rows 2 to 16: 1 ch (does not count as st throughout), 1 sc in each st across, turn.

Fasten off, cut yarn leaving a long tail for sewing. Sew collar to bottom of donut leaving enough room for collar to hang slightly.

COLLAR TAG

Using 3mm hook and lavender, make a magic ring.

Round 1: 6 sc into ring. (6 sts)

Round 2: 2 sc in each st around. (12 sts)

Round 3: [1 sc, 2 sc in next st] 6 times. (18 sts)

Slst in next st, fasten off, cut yarn, leaving a long tail for sewing. Sew collar tag to centre of the cat collar.

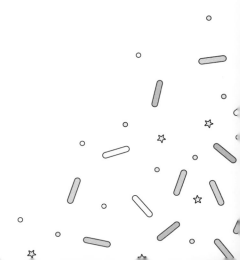

Moose

Playtime with your moose Donut Buddy will involve lots of races as he loves to run around with his friends! You can find him down by the river munching on tasty leaves and twigs!

YOU WILL NEED

- Size 2.5mm (US B/1), 3mm (US C/2 or D/3) and 4mm (US G/6) hooks

- DK or worsted/Aran weight yarn in cream, walnut and parchment

- Embroidery thread in beige and white

- Donut making kit list (see **Basic Donut Pattern**)

- Safety eyes, 2 x 10-14mm*, or black yarn or black embroidery thread to make your own

*Safety eyes should **only** be used for children aged three years or older.

Stuff and sew the small horn onto the large horn before sewing it onto the moose to make it easier to assemble.

DONUT

Follow the **Basic Donut Pattern** to create the donut base in cream and the icing in walnut, omitting the sprinkles. If using safety eyes, place between rounds 4 and 5 of the icing.

EYES

If using safety eyes, these will already have been placed when making the head. Alternatively, to make the toy suitable for children under three years of age, you can crochet or embroider the eyes (see **Basic Donut Pattern: Eyes**). Using a darning needle and white embroidery thread, add a line around one side of each eye. Fasten off at the back and weave in ends.

LARGE ANTLERS (MAKE 2)

Using 2.5mm hook and parchment, make a magic ring.

Round 1: 6 sc into ring. (6 sts)

Round 2: 2 sc in each st around. (12 sts)

Round 3: [1 sc, 2 sc in next st] 6 times. (18 sts)

Rounds 4 to 11: 1 sc in each st around.

Round 12: Inv dec, 6 sc, 2 sc in next 2 sts, 6 sc, inv dec. (18 sts)

Rounds 13 to 21: Rep round 12.

Slst in next st, fasten off, cut yarn, leaving a long tail for sewing. Lightly stuff.

MEDIUM ANTLERS (MAKE 2)

Round 1: 6 sc into ring. (6 sts)

Round 2: 2 sc in each st around. (12 sts)

Round 3: [5 sc, 2 sc in next st] twice. (14 sts)

Rounds 4 to 6: 1 sc in each st around.

Slst in next st, fasten off, cut yarn, leaving a long tail for sewing. Lightly stuff and sew it onto the larger antler. Attach the antlers just behind the icing, evenly spaced apart.

EARS (MAKE 2)

Using 3mm hook and walnut, make a magic ring.

Round 1: 6 sc into ring. (6 sts)

Round 2: [1 sc, 2 sc in next st] 3 times. (9 sts)

Round 3: 1 sc in each st around. (9 sts)

Round 4: [2 sc, 2 sc in next st] 3 times. (12 sts)

Round 5: [3 sc, 2 sc in next st] 3 times. (15 sts)

Rounds 6 to 7: 1 sc in each st around.

Slst in next st, fasten off, cut yarn, leaving a long tail for sewing. Attach ears on each side of the donut hole, just in front of the antlers, evenly spaced apart.

MOUTH

Using 3mm hook and walnut, make a magic ring.

Round 1: 6 sc into ring. (6 sts)

Round 2: 2 sc in each st around. (12 sts)

Round 3: [1 sc, 2 sc in next st] 6 times. (18 sts)

Round 4: [2 sc, 2 sc in next st] 6 times. (24 sts)

Round 5: [3 sc, 2 sc in next st] 6 times. (30 sts)

Rounds 6 to 7: 1 sc in each st around.

Round 8: [3 sc, inv dec] 6 times. (24 sts)

Rounds 9 to 10: 1 sc in each st around.

Slst in next st, fasten off, cut yarn, leaving a long tail for sewing. Lightly stuff and attach mouth central to the donut ring hole, adding two nostril lines with beige embroidery thread one stitch wide by one stitch long.

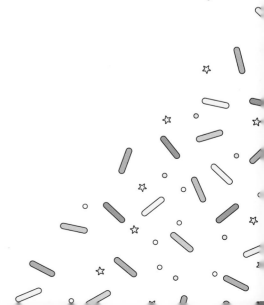

Frog

Ribbit, ribbit! This cute Donut Buddy loves hanging out by the pond. Crochet a few frogs in different shades of green to give him some lily-pad pals!

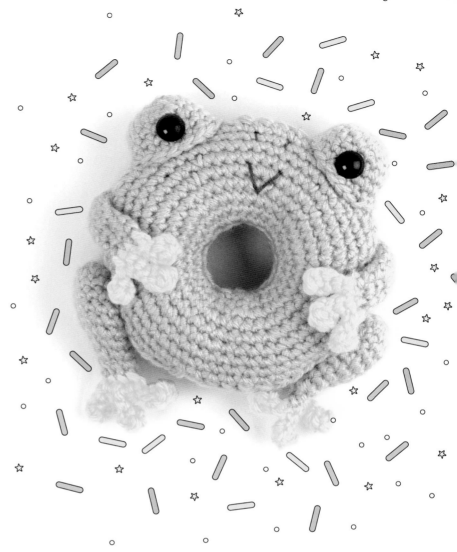

YOU WILL NEED

- Size 2.5mm (US B/1), 3mm (US C/2 or D/3) and 4mm (US G/6) hooks

- DK or worsted/Aran weight yarn in apple green, grass green and citron

- Embroidery thread in grey and pink

- Donut making kit list (see **Basic Donut Pattern**)

- Safety eyes, 2 x 10–14mm*, or black yarn or black embroidery thread to make your own

  *Safety eyes should **only** be used for children aged three years or older.*

DONUT

Follow the **Basic Donut Pattern** to create the donut base in apple green and the icing in grass green, omitting the sprinkles.

EYES (MAKE 2)

Using 3mm hook and grass green, make a magic ring.

Round 1: 6 sc into ring. (6 sts)

Round 2: 2 sc in each st around. (12 sts)

Round 3: [1 sc, 2 sc in next st] 6 times. (18 sts)

Rounds 4 to 6: 1 sc in each st around.

Slst in next st, fasten off, cut yarn, leaving a long tail for sewing. Lightly stuff. Attach the safety eyes between rounds 4 and 5. Alternatively, to make the toy suitable for children under three years of age, crochet or embroider the eyes (see **Basic Donut Pattern: Eyes**). Lightly stuff and attach the eyes, evenly spaced apart. Sew small sprinkle lines just under each eye using pink embroidery thread.

MOUTH & NOSTRILS

Sew a small V-shaped smile between rounds 4 and 5 of the icing and nostrils above using grey embroidery thread.

ARMS & FINGERS (MAKE 2)

Using 3mm hook and grass green, make a magic ring, leaving a long tail at the beginning for sewing.

Round 1: 6 sc into ring. (6 sts)

Rounds 2 to 9: 1 sc in each st around.

Round 10: Folding the arm in half; 3 sc in front and back sts together. (3 sts)

Change to 2.5mm hook and citron to work fingers, make 4 ch.

Row 1: *working in 2nd ch from hook, yo, pull up a loop, yo over and pull through 2 loops on hook, yo, insert hook into same st, yo, pull up a loop, yo, pull through all 4 loops on hook (this creates a small bobble at the end of the finger), slst in next ch, 1 sc in next ch **, 1 sc in next st from round 10, make 4 ch; rep from * for the next 2 fingers, ending last rep at **.

Fasten off, cut yarn and weave in ends. Attach arms on each side of donut, evenly spaced apart.

LEGS & TOES (MAKE 2)

Using 3mm hook and grass green, make a magic ring, leaving a long tail at the beginning for sewing.

Round 1: 8 sc into ring. (8 sts)

Round 2: 2 sc in each st around. (16 sts)

Rounds 3 to 5: 1 sc in each st around.

Round 6: [6 sc, inv dec] twice. (14 sts)

Round 7: [5 sc, inv dec] twice. (12 sts)

Round 8: [4 sc, inv dec] twice. (10 sts)

Lightly stuff the leg.

Round 9: [3 sc, inv dec] twice. (8 sts)

Round 10: [2 sc, inv dec] twice. (6 sts)

Round 11: Folding the leg in half; 3 sc in front and back sts together. (3 sts)

Change to 2.5mm hook and citron to work toes, make 4 ch.

Row 1: *working in 2nd ch from hook, yo, pull up a loop, yo over and pull through 2 loops on hook, yo, insert hook into same st, yo, pull up a loop, yo, pull through all 4 loops on hook (this creates a small bobble at the end of the toe), slst in next ch, 1 sc in next ch **,

1 sc in next st from round 11, make 4 ch; rep from * for the next 2 toes, ending last rep at **.

Fasten off, cut yarn and weave in ends. Attach the legs on each side of the donut, spaced evenly apart.

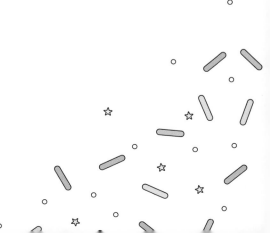

Spider

This incy wincy Donut Buddy loves whipping up a web or two! Catch him out with his friends at the park on a sunny day, or playing in the grass at night!

YOU WILL NEED

- Size 2.5mm (US B/1), 3mm (US C/2 or D/3) and 4mm (US G/6) hooks

- DK or worsted/Aran weight yarn in parma violet, black and white

- Embroidery thread in white

- Donut making kit list (see **Basic Donut Pattern**)

- Safety eyes, 2 x 6mm and 2 x 8mm*, or black yarn or black embroidery thread to make your own

*Safety eyes should **only** be used for children aged three years or older.*

DONUT

Follow the **Basic Donut Pattern** to create the donut base in parma violet and the icing in black, omitting the sprinkles.

WEB

Using white embroidery thread and a darning needle, evenly section the donut into 4 quarters [A]. Add a line between each quarter to create 8 segments [B].

Sew around the donut on rounds 4 and 8 to create the circles on the web [C], fasten off at the back of the icing to secure.

LEGS (MAKE 8)

Using 3mm hook and black, make a magic ring.

Round 1: 6 sc into ring. (6 sts)

Rounds 2 to 3: 1 sc in each st around.

Change to white.

Rounds 4 to 5: 1 sc in each st around.

Change to black.

Rounds 6 to 7: 1 sc in each st around.

Change to white.

Rounds 8 to 9: 1 sc in each st around.

Change to black.

Rounds 10 to 12: 1 sc in each st around.

Fasten off, cut yarn leaving a long tail for sewing. Lightly stuff and attach 4 legs on either side of donut, evenly spaced apart.

HEAD

Using 3mm hook and parma violet make a magic ring.

Round 1: 6 sc into ring. (6 sts)

Round 2: 2 sc in each st around. (12 sts)

Round 3: [1 sc, 2 sc in next st] 6 times. (18 sts)

Round 4: [2 sc, 2 sc in next st] 6 times. (24 sts)

Round 5: [3 sc, 2 sc in next st] 6 times. (30 sts)

Place 8mm safety eyes between rounds 4 and 5.

Round 6: [4 sc, 2 sc in next st] 6 times. (36 sts)

Rounds 7 to 12: 1 sc in each st around.

Place 6mm safety eyes between rounds 6 and 7.

Round 13: [4 sc, inv dec] 6 times. (30 sts)

Round 14: [3 sc, inv dec] 6 times. (24 sts)

Stuff head firmly.

Round 15: [2 sc, inv dec] 6 times. (18 sts)

Add a little more stuffing.

Round 16: [1 sc, inv dec] 6 times. (12 sts)

Round 17: [Inv dec] 6 times.

Fasten off, cut yarn, leaving a long tail for sewing. Attach head to donut body.

EYES

If using safety eyes, these will already have been placed when making the head. Alternatively, to make the toy suitable for children under three years of age, crochet or embroider the eyes (see **Basic Donut Pattern: Eyes**). For the larger eyes work 5 sc into a ring instead of 4 sc.

FANGS (MAKE 2)

Using 2.5mm hook and black make a magic ring.

Round 1: 4 sc into ring. (4 sts)

Rounds 2 to 4: 1 sc in each st around.

Slst, fasten off, cut yarn leaving a long tail for sewing. Attach fangs below eyes, evenly spaced apart.

A

B

C

Stegosaurus

This ancient Donut Buddy loves to roam amongst the trees with his dino-pals. His bright colours help him to stand out from the crowd!

YOU WILL NEED

- Size 2.5mm (US B/1), 3mm (US C/2 or D/3) and 4mm (US G/6) hooks
- DK or worsted/Aran weight yarn in lime, royal blue and orange
- 4-ply cotton yarn in white
- Donut making kit list (see **Basic Donut Pattern**)
- Safety eyes, 2 x 10–14mm*, or black yarn or black embroidery thread to make your own

*Safety eyes should **only** be used for children aged three years or older.*

DONUT

Follow the **Basic Donut Pattern** to create the donut base in lime and the icing in royal blue. Add white sprinkles over the top third of the donut as in the photo.

HEAD

Using 3mm hook and lime, make a magic ring.

Round 1: 6 sc into ring. (6 sts)

Round 2: 2 sc in each st around. (12 sts)

Round 3: [1 sc, 2 sc in next st] 6 times. (18 sts)

Round 4: [2 sc, 2 sc in next st] 6 times. (24 sts)

Round 5: [3 sc, 2 sc in next st] 6 times. (30 sts)

Rounds 6 to 10: 1 sc in each st around.

Place safety eyes between rounds 7 and 8.

Round 11: [3 sc, inv dec] 6 times. (24 sts)

Round 12: [2 sc, inv dec] 6 times. (18 sts)

Round 13: 1 sc in each st around. (18 sts)

Round 14: 1 sc into first st, inv dec into next st, repeat all around. (12 sts)

Slst in next st, fasten off, cut yarn leaving a long tail for sewing. Stuff the head firmly. Attach head to donut body.

SPIKES (MAKE 6)

Using 2.5mm hook and orange make a magic ring.

Round 1: 6 sc into ring. (6 sts)

Round 2: [2 sc, 2 sc in next st] twice. (8 sts)

Round 3: [3 sc, 2 sc in next st] twice. (10 sts)

Round 4: [4 sc, 2 sc in next st] twice. (12 sts)

Round 5: [5 sc, 2 sc in next st] twice. (14 sts)

Slst, fasten off, cut yarn, leaving a long tail for sewing. Attach the spikes in two lines, placing one in front of the other in a staggered shape.

TAIL

Using 3mm hook and lime, make a magic ring.

Round 1: 6 sc into ring. (6 sts)

Round 2: 1 sc in each st around.

Round 3: 3 sc, 2 sc in next st, 2 sc. (7 sts)

Round 4: 1 sc in each st around.

Round 5: 3 sc, 2 sc in next st, 3 sc. (8 sts)

Round 6: 1 sc in each st around.

Round 7: 3 sc, 2 sc in next st, 4 sc. (9 sts)

Round 8: 1 sc in each st around.

Round 9: 3 sc, 2 sc in next st, 5 sc. (10 sts)

Round 10: 3 sc, 2 sc in next st, 6 sc. (11 sts)

Round 11: 3 sc, 2 sc in next st, 7 sc. (12 sts)

Round 12: 3 sc, 2 sc in next st, 8 sc. (13 sts)

Slst, fasten off, cut yarn, leaving a long tail for sewing. Lightly stuff, then attach tail to other end of donut from head.

TAIL SPIKES (MAKE 2)

Using 2.5mm hook and orange make a magic ring.

Round 1: 6 sc into ring. (6 sts)

Round 2: 1 sc in each st around.

Slst, fasten off, cut yarn, leaving a long tail for sewing. Attach to top of tail near the end.

LEGS (MAKE 2)

Using 3mm hook and royal blue, make a magic ring.

Round 1: 6 sc into ring. (6 sts)

Round 2: 2 sc in each st around. (12 sts)

Round 3: [1 sc, 2 sc in next st] 6 times. (18 sts)

Change to orange.

Round 4: working into the blo (see **Crochet Techniques**); 1 sc in each st around.

Change to lime.

Round 5: 1 sc in each st around.

Round 6: [1 sc, inv dec] 6 times. (12 sts)

Rounds 7 to 8: 1 sc in each st around.

Slst, fasten off, cut yarn, leaving a long tail for sewing. Lightly stuff and then sew on each leg, one in line with the head and the other in line with the base of the tail.

EYES

If using safety eyes, these will already have been placed when making the head. Alternatively, to make the toy suitable for children under three years of age, you can crochet or embroider the eyes (see **Basic Donut Pattern: Eyes**).

Star

Twinkle, twinkle, little star, how I wonder what you are! Well you're a sparkling Donut Buddy of course! This bright lady is wide awake at night and spends her days dreaming of playtime.

YOU WILL NEED

- Size 3mm (US C/2 or D/3) and 4mm (US G/6) hooks

- DK or worsted/Aran weight yarn in yellow

- 4-ply cotton yarn in pink

- Embroidery thread in pink

- Donut making kit list (see **Basic Donut Pattern**)

- Safety eyes, 2 x 10–14mm*, or black yarn or black embroidery thread to make your own

*Safety eyes should **only** be used for children aged three years or older.*

Mark each point evenly with a pin in the donut before sewing to make it easier to sew together.

DONUT

Follow the **Basic Donut Pattern** to create the donut base and the icing in yellow omitting the sprinkles. If using safety eyes, place between rounds 4 and 5 of the icing.

LARGE STAR POINTS (MAKE 3)

Using 3mm hook and yellow make a magic ring.

Round 1: 6 sc into ring. (6 sts)

Round 2: [1 sc, 2 sc in next st] 3 times. (9 sts)

Round 3: 1 sc in each st around.

Round 4: [2 sc, 2 sc in next st] 3 times. (12 sts)

Round 5: [1 sc, 2 sc in next st] 6 times. (18 sts)

Round 6: 1 sc in each st around.

Round 7: [2 sc, 2 sc in next st] 6 times. (24 sts)

Round 8: 1 sc in each st around.

Round 9: [3 sc, 2 sc in next st] 6 times. (30 sts)

Round 10: 1 sc in each st around.

Slst, fasten off, cut yarn, leaving a long tail for sewing.

SMALL STAR POINTS (MAKE 2)

Using 3mm hook and yellow, make a magic ring.

Round 1: 6 sc into ring. (6 sts)

Round 2: [1 sc, 2 sc in next st] 3 times. (9 sts)

Round 3: 1 sc in each st around.

Round 4: [2 sc, 2 sc in next st] 3 times. (12 sts)

Round 5: [1 sc, 2 sc in next st] 6 times. (18 sts)

Round 6: 1 sc in each st around.

Round 7: [2 sc, 2 sc in next st] 6 times. (24 sts)

Round 8: 1 sc in each st around.

Slst, fasten off, cut yarn, leaving a long tail for sewing. Lightly stuff, then attach the star points with one of the largest points at the top and alternating the rest.

EYES

If using safety eyes, these will already have been placed when making the donut. Alternatively, to make the toy suitable for children under three years of age, you can crochet or embroider the eyes (see **Basic Donut Pattern: Eyes**).

CHEEKS (MAKE 2)

Using 3mm hook and pink make a magic ring.

Round 1: 4 sc into ring. (4 sts)

Slst, fasten off, cut yarn, leaving a long tail for sewing. Attach the cheeks just below and to the side of the eyes.

MOUTH

Make a V-shape mouth between the cheeks and eyes using pink embroidery thread.

Rhino

This little buddy isn't scared to take charge. With his bright pointy horn, he's sure to turn heads while munching on tasty leaves in the hot savannah sun!

YOU WILL NEED

- Size 2.5mm (US B/1), 3mm (US C/2 or D/3) and 4mm (US G/6) hooks

- DK or worsted/Aran weight yarn in light grey, dark grey, white and pink

- Embroidery thread in white

- Donut making kit list (see **Basic Donut Pattern**)

- Safety eyes, 2 x 10–14mm*, or black yarn or black embroidery thread to make your own

*Safety eyes should **only** be used for children aged three years or older.*

Stuff and sew your horns onto the rhino nose before stuffing and sewing the nose onto the donut.

DONUT

Follow the **Basic Donut Pattern** to create the donut base in light grey and the icing in dark grey, omitting the sprinkles. If using safety eyes, place between rounds 4 and 5 of the icing.

INNER EARS (MAKE 2)

Using 2.5mm hook and pink, make a magic ring.

Round 1: 6 sc into ring. (6 sts)

Round 2: 2 sc in each st around. (12 sts)

Slst, fasten off, cut yarn, leaving a long tail for sewing.

OUTER EARS (MAKE 2)

Using 2.5mm hook and dark grey, make a magic ring.

Round 1: 6 sc into ring. (6 sts)

Round 2: 2 sc in each st around. (12 sts)

Round 3: [1 sc, 2 sc in next st] 6 times. (18 sts)

Slst, fasten off, cut yarn, leaving a long tail for sewing. Sew inner ears inside outer ears as in photo. Attach each ear on side of donut hole, at the back of the icing, evenly spaced apart, by folding over the circle and pinching the ends together to make a curved shape. Sew the bottom 3 sts closed to complete.

MUZZLE

Using 3mm hook and dark grey, make a magic ring.

Round 1: 6 sc into ring. (6 sts)

Round 2: 2 sc in each st around. (12 sts)

Round 3: [1 sc, 2 sc in next st] 6 times. (18 sts)

Round 4: 1 sc in each st around.

Round 5: [2 sc, 2 sc in next st] 6 times. (24 sts)

Rounds 6 to 7: 1 sc in each st around.

Round 8: [2 sc, inv dec] 6 times. (18 sts)

Slst, fasten off, cut yarn, leaving a long tail for sewing.

LARGE HORN

Using 3mm hook and white, make a magic ring.

Round 1: 4 sc into ring. (4 sts)

Round 2: [1 sc, 2 sc in next st] twice. (6 sts)

Round 3: [2 sc, 2 sc in next st] twice. (8 sts)

Round 4: [3 sc, 2 sc in next st] twice. (10 sts)

Round 5: [4 sc, 2 sc in next st] twice. (12 sts)

Round 6: [5 sc, 2 sc in next st] twice. (14 sts)

Slst, fasten off, cut yarn, leaving a long tail for sewing.

SMALL HORN

Using 3mm hook and white, make a magic ring.

Round 1: 4 sc into ring. (4 sts)

Round 2: [1 sc, 2 sc in next st] twice. (6 sts)

Round 3: 1 sc in each st around.

Slst, fasten off, cut yarn, leaving a long tail for sewing. Lightly stuff and attach both horns to muzzle, with the bigger horn at the front. Lightly stuff the muzzle and attach central to donut ring hole.

EYES

If using safety eyes, these will already have been placed when making the donut. Alternatively, to make the toy suitable for children under three years of age, you can crochet or embroider the eyes (see **Basic Donut Pattern: Eyes**). Add a line of white embroidery thread to the outside edge of each eye with a darning needle.

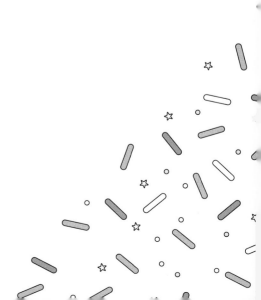

Pig

Oink, oink! This friendly Donut Pal loves rolling around on the farmyard and getting muddy with her friends. The cows, horses and chickens love hanging out with her at playtime on the farm!

YOU WILL NEED

- Size 3mm (US C/2 or D/3) and 4mm (US G/6) hooks

- DK or worsted/Aran weight yarn in rose and pale pink

- Embroidery thread in white and coral

- Donut making kit list (see **Basic Donut Pattern**)

- Safety eyes, 2 x 10–14mm*, or black yarn or black embroidery thread to make your own

*Safety eyes should **only** be used for children aged three years or older.

Add the bow in the top corner of the ear or just below the nose to create a bow tie, or why not mix and match and add a flower – the choice is yours!

DONUT

Follow the **Basic Donut Pattern** to create the donut base in rose and the icing in pale pink, omitting the sprinkles. If using safety eyes, place between rounds 4 and 5 of the icing.

EARS (MAKE 2)

Using 3mm hook and pale pink, make a magic ring.

Round 1: 6 sc into ring. (6 sts)

Round 2: [1 sc, 2 sc in next st] 3 times. (9 sts)

Round 3: 1 sc in each st around.

Round 4: [2 sc, 2 sc in next st] 3 times. (12 sts)

Round 5: 1 sc in each st around.

Round 6: [3 sc, 2 sc in next st] 3 times. (15 sts)

Round 7: [4 sc, 2 sc in next st] 3 times. (18 sts)

Rounds 8 to 9: 1 sc in each st around.

Round 10: Folding the ear in half, slst across the end to close.

Fasten off, cut yarn, leaving a long tail for sewing. Attach ears to the donut, evenly spaced apart, at the back of the icing.

SNOUT

Using 3mm hook and pale pink, make a magic ring.

Round 1: 6 sc into ring. (6 sts)

Round 2: [3 sc in the next st, 2 sc] twice. (10 sts)

Round 3: [1 sc, 2 sc in next st] 5 times. (15 sts)

Round 4: 2 sc, 2 sc in next st, 3 sc in next st, 5 sc, 3 sc in next st, 2 sc in next st, 4 sc. (21 sts)

Round 5: 1 sc blo (see **Crochet Techniques**) in each st around.

Round 6: 1 sc in each st around.

Slst, fasten off, cut yarn, leaving a long tail for sewing. Stuff lightly. Attach to donut icing just under the donut hole in the centre. Using coral embroidery thread, sew two small lines for nostrils.

EYES

If using safety eyes, these will already have been placed when making the donut. Alternatively, to make the toy suitable for children under three years of age, you can crochet or embroider the eyes (see **Basic Donut Pattern: Eyes**). Add a line of white embroidery thread to the outside edge of each eye with a darning needle.

FINISHING TOUCHES

To add a bow to your pig, make one in coral (see **Accessories**), then sew securely to bottom of one of the ears.

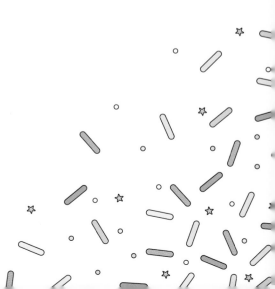

Turkey

How magnificent does this turkey look? With his beautiful plumage and colourful chest, he's ready for autumn! Catch him showing off his glorious colours to his Donut Buddy pals!

YOU WILL NEED

- Size 2.5mm (US B/1), 3mm (US C/2 or D/3) and 4mm (US G/6) hooks

- DK or worsted/Aran weight yarn in walnut, brown, yellow, beige, red and orange

- Embroidery thread in white, pale blue, mid blue and dark blue

- Donut making kit list (see **Basic Donut Pattern**)

- Safety eyes, 2 x 10–14mm*, or black yarn or black embroidery thread to make your own

*Safety eyes should **only** be used for children aged three years or older.

Embroider the flecks of colour onto the turkey one stitch wide, leaving 1 row before you add your next colour.

DONUT

Follow the **Basic Donut Pattern** to create the donut base and the icing in walnut, omitting the sprinkles. If using safety eyes, place between rounds 4 and 5 of the icing.

PLUMAGE

Using 4mm hook and beige, make 26 ch.

Row 1: starting in the 2nd ch from hook, 1 hdc in each st across, turn. (25 sts)

Row 2: 1 ch (does not count as st here and throughout), 2 hdc in the first st, 3 hdc, [2 hdc in the next st, 3 hdc] 5 times, 2 hdc in last st, turn. (32 sts)

Change to orange.

Row 3: 1 ch, 2 hdc in the first st, 3 hdc, [2 hdc in the next st, 3 hdc] 7 times, turn. (40 sts)

Row 4: 1 ch, 1 sc in each st across, turn.

Change to brown.

Round 5: 1 ch, 1 hdc in each st across, fasten off.

PLUMAGE FRILL

Using 4mm hook and beige and red held together, attach yarn to first st of plumage, 1 ch.

Row 1: 1 sc in first st, 5 dc in next st (shell st – see **Techniques**), [1 sc, 1 shell st] 18 times. (19 shells sts)

Fasten off, cut yarn, leaving a long tail for sewing. Sew the plumage at the back of the donut securely so that the top of the frill is slightly above the donut.

EYES

If using safety eyes, these will already have been placed when making the donut. Alternatively, to make the toy suitable for children under three years of age, you can crochet or embroider the eyes (see **Basic Donut Pattern: Eyes**). Add a line of white embroidery thread to the outside edge of each eye with a darning needle.

BEAK

Using 3mm hook and yellow make a magic ring.

Round 1: 6 sc into ring. (6 sts)

Round 2: [1 sc, 2 sc in next st] 3 times. (9 sts)

Rounds 3 to 4: 1 sc in each st around.

Slst, fasten off, cut yarn, leaving a long tail for sewing. Stuff lightly and attach to donut.

SNOOD (MAKE 2)

Using 3mm hook and red, make a magic ring.

Round 1: 4 sc into ring. (4 sts)

Rounds 2 to 4: 1 sc in each st around.

Slst, fasten off, cut yarn, leaving a long tail for sewing. Lightly stuff, then attach snoods on either side of beak.

TOES (MAKE 4)

Using 2.5mm hook and yellow, make a magic ring.

Round 1: 6 sc into ring. (6 sts)

Round 2: [1 sc, 2 sc in next st] 3 times. (9 sts)

Rounds 3 to 5: 1 sc in each st around.

Fasten off first 2 toes only and weave in ends. Continue to feet.

Round 6: Pulling both toes together 3 sc across sts in both toes to join, 12 sc in rest of sts. (12 sts, joined sts do not form part of st count).

Rounds 7 to 8: 1 sc in each st around.

Slst, fasten off, cut yarn, leaving a long tail for sewing. Lightly stuff, then attach at the bottom of donut.

WINGS (MAKE 2)

Using 4mm hook and beige and red held together, make a magic ring.

Round 1: 6 sc into ring. (6 sts)

Round 2: 2 sc in each st around. (12 sts)

Round 3: [1 sc, 2 sc in next st] 6 times. (18 sts)

Round 4: 6 sc, 5 ch, sc in next sc, 10 ch, sc in next sc, 15 ch, sc in next sc, 10 ch, sc in next sc, 5 ch, sc in next sc, 7 sc.

Fasten off, cut yarn, leaving a long tail for sewing. Attach each wing to side of donut just under the plumage.

Using shades of blue embroidery thread, sew small lines on the front of the body to create a pretty front panel as shown.

Ladybug

1 spot, 2 spot, 3 spot, 4! Ladybug loves to count them all! She also loves playing in the garden with her insect friends. Have fun making this Donut Pal in an array of bright colours.

YOU WILL NEED

- Size 3mm (US C/2 or D/3) and 4mm (US G/6) hooks

- DK or worsted/Aran weight yarn in black and red

- Donut making kit list (see **Basic Donut Pattern**)

Add as many spots as you like to make it your own, why not try different coloured spots for a fun learning experience.

DONUT

Follow the **Basic Donut Pattern** to create the donut base in black and the icing in red, omitting the sprinkles. No eyes are needed for this donut.

CENTRE LINES (MAKE 2)

Using 3mm hook and black, make 13 ch.

Fasten off, cut yarn, leaving a long tail for sewing. Attach each line across centre of donut from end of icing on the outside to middle of donut, opposite each other as shown.

SPOTS (MAKE 6)

Using 3mm hook and black, make a magic ring.

Round 1: 6 sc into ring. (6 sts)

Slst, fasten off, cut yarn, leaving a long tail for sewing. Attach 3 spots each side of the central line evenly.

HEAD

Using 3mm hook and black, make a magic ring.

Round 1: 6 sc into ring. (6 sts)

Round 2: 2 sc in each st around. (12 sts)

Round 3: [1 sc, 2 sc in next st] 6 times. (18 sts)

Round 4: [2 sc, 2 sc in next st] 6 times. (24 sts)

Round 5: 1 sc in each st around.

Rounds 6 to 7: 1 sc in each st around.

Slst, fasten off, cut yarn, leaving a long tail for sewing. Lightly stuff and attach the head to the donut by folding the half circle and stitching half onto the edge of the icing and half onto the base, being careful not to flatten the head.

ANTENNAE (MAKE 2)

Using 3mm hook and black, make 6 ch.

Row 1: 1 hdc in 2nd ch from hook, to form a ball shape at the tip, slst in next st.

Fasten off, cut yarn, leaving a long tail for sewing. Attach on either side of the centre of the head.

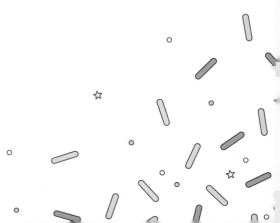

Koala

Koala loves to sleep all day, dreaming of eucalyptus leaves! Spend some koality-time with this cuddly Donut Buddy this weekend! Look how soft and snuggly his ears are.

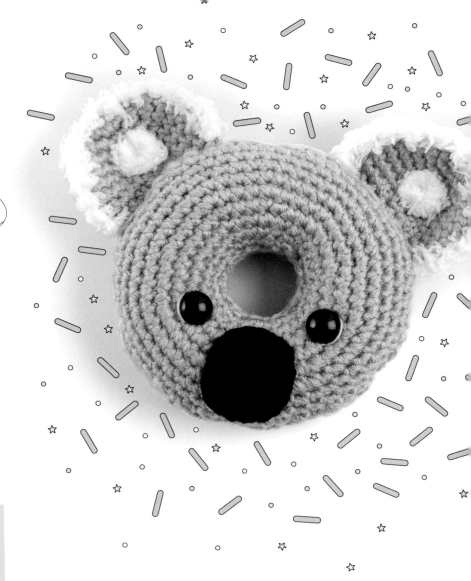

YOU WILL NEED

- Size 3mm (US C/2 or D/3) and 4mm (US G/6) hooks

- DK or worsted/Aran weight yarn in black and grey

- Any weight fluffy or eyelash yarn in white

- Embroidery thread in white

- Donut making kit list (see **Basic Donut Pattern**)

- Safety eyes, 2 x 10–14mm*, or black yarn or black embroidery thread to make your own

*Safety eyes should **only** be used for children aged three years or older.*

DONUT

Follow the **Basic Donut Pattern** to create the donut base and the icing in grey, omitting the sprinkles. If using safety eyes, place between rounds 4 and 5 of the icing.

EARS (MAKE 2)

Using 4mm hook and grey, make a magic ring.

Round 1: 6 sc into ring. (6 sts)

Round 2: 2 sc in each st around. (12 sts)

Round 3: [1 sc, 2 sc in next st] 6 times. (18 sts)

Round 4: [2 sc, 2 sc in next st] 6 times. (24 sts)

Rounds 5 to 8: 1 sc in each st around.

Round 9: 1 sc into first 2 sts, inv dec into next st; repeat all around, slst in next st, fasten off, cut yarn, leaving a long tail for sewing. (18 sts)

Change to white eyelash yarn.

Round 10: Folding the ear in half [A], insert hook into the side of the ear and work 1 ch 1 [B], [sc in next st, 1 ch] to end [C], fasten off and weave in ends [D].

MIDDLE EARS (MAKE 2)

Using 3mm hook and white eyelash yarn, make a magic ring.

Round 1: 3 sc into ring. (3 sts)

Round 2: 2 sc in each st around. (6 sts)

Round 3: [1 sc, 2 sc in next st] 3 times. (9 sts)

Slst, fasten off, cut yarn, leaving a long tail for sewing. Attach each ear to the donut each side of hole at back of icing, then attach middle ears.

EYES

If using safety eyes, these will already have been placed when making the donut. Alternatively, to make the toy suitable for children under three years of age, you can crochet or embroider the eyes (see **Basic Donut Pattern: Eyes**). Add a line of white embroidery thread to the outside edge of each eye with a darning needle.

NOSE

Using 3mm hook and black, make 5 ch.

Round 1: 2 sc in 2nd ch from hook, 2 sc, 5 sc in next st, working on opposite side of ch, 3 sc. (12 sts)

Round 2: 2 sc in next 3 sts, [2 sc, 2 sc in next st] 3 times. (18 sts)

Rounds 3 to 4: 1 sc in each st around.

Slst, fasten off, cut yarn, leaving a long tail for sewing. Lightly stuff and attach to donut, making sure it lines up with centre of donut hole.

A

B

C

D

Pumpkin

Pumpkin Donut Buddy loves the change of season and is so looking forward to autumn. He's a firm favourite, taking pride of place in any home on Halloween night!

YOU WILL NEED

- Size 3mm (US C/2 or D/3) and 4mm (US G/6) hooks
- DK or worsted/Aran weight yarn in orange, green, pink and brown
- Embroidery thread in white and dark orange
- Donut making kit list (see **Basic Donut Pattern**)
- Safety eyes, 2 x 10–14mm*, or black yarn or black embroidery thread to make your own

*Safety eyes should **only** be used for children aged three years or older.

Overlap the leaves slightly before sewing them onto your pumpkin. Create lots of autumnal colours for a fun feel.

DONUT

Follow the **Basic Donut Pattern** to create the donut base and the icing in orange, omitting the sprinkles. If using safety eyes, place between rounds 6 and 7 of the icing.

LINES

Using a darning needle and orange, evenly segment the donut into 5 parts. Insert needle into back of donut at a point along the centre, wrap yarn around front of icing, pull tightly and insert needle through same place, thread yarn through fabric to back of next segment and wrap around front of icing again in same way. Repeat 3 more times, knot the yarn tightly, fasten off, cut yarn, and weave in ends.

EYES

If using safety eyes, these will already have been placed when making the donut. Alternatively, to make the toy suitable for children under three years of age, you can crochet or embroider the eyes (see **Basic Donut Pattern: Eyes**). Add a line of white embroidery thread to the outside edge of each eye with a darning needle.

MOUTH

Using dark orange, sew a V-shape smile in the icing, just below the donut hole.

STALK

Using 3mm hook and brown, make a magic ring.

Round 1: 6 sc into ring. (6 sts)

Rounds 2 to 5: 1 sc in each st around.

Slst, fasten off, cut yarn, leaving a long tail for sewing. Attach in centre of top of donut hole at back of icing.

LEAVES (MAKE 2)

Using 3mm hook and green, make a magic ring.

Round 1: 2 ch, 6dc in ring, 3 ch, slst in 3rd ch from hook, 6 dc in ring, 2 ch, slst into top of first 2 ch.

Fasten off, cut yarn, leaving a long tail for sewing. Attach as shown, overlapping each other.

CURLY TENDRIL

Using 3mm hook and brown make 16 ch.

Row 1: 3 sc in 2nd ch from hook and in each st across.

Fasten off, cut yarn, leaving a long tail for sewing. Attach on opposite side of stalk to the leaves.

CHEEKS (MAKE 2)

Using 3mm hook and pink, make a magic ring.

Round 1: 5 sc into ring. (5 sts)

Slst, fasten off, cut yarn, leaving a long tail for sewing. Attach the cheeks just below and to the side of each eye.

Fish

With her beautiful trailing tails and vibrant colours, this fish looks stylish swimming in the seas! Make multiple fish in a variety of bold colours to create a whole aquarium!

YOU WILL NEED

- Size 3mm (US C/2 or D/3) and 4mm (US G/6) hooks

- DK or worsted/Aran weight yarn in spearmint, kingfisher blue and shrimp

- Donut making kit list (see **Basic Donut Pattern**)

- Safety eyes, 2 x 10–14mm*, or black yarn or black embroidery thread to make your own

*Safety eyes should **only** be used for children aged three years or older.*

DONUT

Follow the **Basic Donut Pattern** to create the donut base and the icing in spearmint, omitting the sprinkles.

HEAD

Using 4mm hook and spearmint, make a magic ring.

Round 1: 6 sc into ring. (6 sts)

Round 2: [1 sc, 2 sc in next st] 3 times. (9 sts)

Round 3: 1 sc in each st around.

Round 4: [2 sc, 2 sc in next st] 3 times. (12 sts)

Round 5: [1 sc, 2 sc in next st] 6 times. (18 sts)

Round 6: 1 sc in each st around.

Change to shrimp and kingfisher blue held together.

Round 7: [2 sc, 2 sc in next st] 6 times. (24 sts)

Place safety eyes between rounds 6 and 7.

Change to spearmint.

Round 8: 1 sc in each st around.

Change to shrimp and kingfisher blue held together.

Round 9: [3 sc, 2 sc in next st] 6 times. (30 sts)

Change to spearmint.

Round 10: 1 sc in each st around.

Slst, fasten off, cut yarn, leaving a long tail for sewing. Attach to one side of donut body on top of icing.

EYES

If using safety eyes, these will already have been placed when making the head. Alternatively, to make the toy suitable for children under three years of age, you can crochet or embroider the eyes (see **Basic Donut Pattern: Eyes**).

PECTORAL SIDE FINS (MAKE 2)

Using 3mm hook and shrimp and kingfisher blue held together, make 9 ch.

Row 1: starting in 2nd ch from hook, 3 hdc in first st, 3 sc, slst in next 2 sts, turn. (8 sts)

Row 2: 1 ch (does not count as st throughout), slst in first 2 sts, 3 sc, 3 hdc, turn.

Row 3: 1 ch, 3 hdc, 3 sc, slst in next 2 sts, turn.

Row 4: 1 ch, slst in first 2 sts, 3 sc, 3 hdc, fasten off, cut yarn, leaving a long tail for sewing. Attach to Donut, lining up with the Donut ring hole as shown.

DORSAL TOP FIN

Using 3mm hook and shrimp and kingfisher blue held together, make 6 ch.

Row 1: starting in 2nd ch from hook, 1 hdc in each st along, turn. (5 sts)

Row 2: 1 ch (does not count as st throughout), 2 hdc, 2 hdc in next st, 2 hdc, turn. (6 sts)

Rows 3 to 4: 1 ch, 1 sc in each st across, turn.

Row 5: 1 ch, 4 hdc, inv dec. (5 sts).

Fasten off, cut yarn, leaving a long tail for sewing. Fold in half, sew the bottom closed, attach to top of donut.

TAIL FIN (MAKE 3, 1 IN EACH COLOUR)

Using 3mm hook, make 38 ch.

Row 1: starting in 2nd ch from hook, 14 hdc, [hdc inv dec] 4 times, 14 hdc, 4 ch, turn. (36 sts)

Row 2: starting in 2nd ch from hook, 14 hdc, [hdc inv dec] 4 times, 13 hdc, 4 ch, turn. (35 sts)

Row 3: starting in 2nd ch from hook, 13 hdc, [hdc inv dec] 4 times, 10 hdc, 1 ch, turn. (28 sts)

Row 4: starting in 2nd ch from hook, 8 hdc, [hdc inv dec] 4 times, 9 hdc. (21 sts)

Fasten off, cut yarn, weave in ends. Overlapping the 3 tail fins (see photo), sew them together, attach to side of the donut lining up with donut ring hole and head.

Hedgehog

This spiky Donut Buddy uses his snout to find his favourite foods in the woodlands. He loves berries and fruit, which he shares with his friends around the campfire!

YOU WILL NEED

- Size 3mm (US C/2 or D/3) and 4mm (US G/6) hooks
- DK or worsted/Aran weight yarn in beige, walnut and black
- Donut making kit list (see **Basic Donut Pattern**)
- Safety eyes, 2 x 10-14mm*, or black yarn or black embroidery thread to make your own

*Safety eyes should **only** be used for children aged three years or older.*

DONUT BASE

Follow the **Basic Donut Pattern** to create the donut base in beige.

ICING

Using 4mm hook and walnut, leaving a long tail for sewing, make 20 ch, join to first ch to make a circle. (20 sts)

Round 1: 1 ch, 1 sc in the same st, 2 sc in next st, [1 sc, 2 sc in next st] 9 times. (30 sts)

Round 2: BS (bobble) in first st (see **Crochet Techniques**), 2 sc, [BS, 2 sc] 9 times.

Round 3: [2 sc, 2 sc in next st] 10 times. (40 sts)

Round 4: [BS, 2 sc] 13 times, 1 sc.

Round 5: [3 sc, 2 sc in next st] 10 times. (50 sts)

Round 6: [BS, 2 sc] 16 times, 2 sc.

Round 7: 1 sc in each st around.

Round 8: [BS, 2 sc] 16 times, 2 sc.

Round 9: (Drip 1) 1 sc, 1 hdc, 1 dc, 1 trc, 1 dc, 1 hdc, 3 sc; (drip 2) 1 hdc, 1 dc, 2 trc, 1 dc, 3 sc; (drip 3) 1 hdc, 2 dc, 1 hdc, 3 sc; (drip 4) 1 hdc, 1 dc, 2 trc, 1 dc, 1 hdc, 3 sc; (drip 5) 1 hdc, 2 dc, 1 trc, 1 dc, 1 hdc, 3 sc; (drip 6) 2 hdc, 3 dc, 3 sc. (50 sts)

Slst in next st, fasten off, cut yarn, leaving a long tail for sewing. Sew the icing to the donut base starting at the hole, then sew around the edge.

HEAD

Using 3mm hook and beige make a magic ring.

Round 1: 4 sc into ring. (4 sts)

Round 2: [1 sc, 2 sc in next st] twice. (6 sts)

Round 3: 2 sc in first 3 sts, 3 sc. (9 sts)

Round 4: 2 sc in first 3 sts, 6 sc. (12 sts)

Round 5: 2 sc in first 3 sts, 9 sc. (15 sts)

Round 6: 2 sc in first 3 sts, 12 sc. (18 sts)

Round 7: 1 sc in each st around.

Attach safety eyes between rounds 6 and 7.

Round 8: [2 sc, 2 sc in next st] 6 times. (24 sts)

Round 9: 1 sc in each st around.

Round 10: [3 sc, 2 sc in next st] 6 times. (30 sts)

Slst in next st, fasten off, cut yarn, leaving a long tail for sewing. Lightly stuff and attach at the front of the donut halfway across the icing and base.

NOSE

Using darning needle and black, thread through tip of nose, weaving back and forth until the area is covered, fasten off and weave in ends.

MOUTH

Using darning needle and black, sew a small line just below nose.

SPIKES

(See **Crochet Techniques: Attaching the Hair** to see the basic technique for attaching the spikes.)

Cut strands of yarn roughly 2cm in length in walnut and beige, thread from back of icing to front making sure to knot the back tightly, all around top of body as shown. Trim to one length.

FEET (MAKE 2)

Using 3mm hook and walnut, make a magic ring.

Round 1: 4 sc into ring. (4 sts)

Round 2: 2 sc in first 2 sts, 2 sc. (6 sts)

Rounds 3 to 4: 1 sc in each st around.

Fasten off, cut yarn, leaving a long tail for sewing. Lightly stuff and attach legs either side of the donut, evenly spaced apart.

TAIL

Using 3mm hook and walnut, make a magic ring.

Round 1: 4 sc into ring. (4 sts)

Rounds 2 to 3: 1 sc in each st around.

Fasten off, cut yarn, leaving a long tail for sewing. Lightly stuff and attach at back of body.

EYES

If using safety eyes, these will already have been placed when making the head. Alternatively, to make the toy suitable for children under three years of age, you can crochet or embroider the eyes (see **Basic Donut Pattern: Eyes**).

Octopus

This octo-pal loves swimming with her sea buddies all day. With her eight arms she can speed past all of her friends at the beach! You'll have great fun stitching this beautiful Donut Buddy!

YOU WILL NEED

- Size 3mm (US C/2 or D/3) and 4mm (US G/6) hooks

- DK or worsted/Aran weight yarn in bright pink and shrimp

- Embroidery thread in white, lavender and orange

- Donut making kit list (see **Basic Donut Pattern**)

- Safety eyes, 2 x 10–14mm*, or black yarn or black embroidery thread to make your own

*Safety eyes should **only** be used for children aged three years or older.

Embroider lots of fun coloured sprinkles on one side of the octopus' face or leave them off – it's up to you!

DONUT

Follow the **Basic Donut Pattern** to create the donut base in bright pink and the icing in shrimp, with sprinkles in shrimp on the base only. If using safety eyes, place between rounds 4 and 5 of the icing.

LARGE TENTACLES (MAKE 4)

Using 3mm hook and shrimp, make 29 ch.

Row 1: starting in 2nd ch from hook, 2 slst, 1 sc, 3 sc in next st, 2 sc, hdc3tog, 5 hdc, 4 hdc in next st, 3 hdc, 4 dc, dc3tog, 3 dc. (29 sts)

Fasten off, cut yarn, leaving a long tail for sewing.

MEDIUM TENTACLES (MAKE 4)

Using 3mm hook and shrimp, make 20 ch.

Row 1: starting in 2nd ch from hook, 2 slst, 1 sc, 3 sc in next st, 2 sc, 1 hdc, hdc3tog, 1 hdc, 2 dc, dc3tog, 3 dc. (17 sts)

Fasten off, cut yarn, leaving a long tail for sewing. Attach two medium tentacles at the front, then alternate between longer and shorter tentacles on the side of the donut.

EYES

If using safety eyes, these will already have been placed when making the donut. Alternatively, to make the toy suitable for children under three years of age, you can crochet or embroider the eyes (see **Basic Donut Pattern: Eyes**). Add a white line around outer half of each eye.

SPRINKLES & MOUTH

Using embroidery thread in white and lavender, add sprinkles to the outer part of one section of the donut, as shown. Add a small V-shaped smile using orange.

Llama

This colourful Llama buddy is ready to party and is always first on the dancefloor! She loves to get dressed up; see her pretty decorated ears and brightly coloured reins!

YOU WILL NEED

- Size 3mm (US C/2 or D/3) and 4mm (US G/6) hooks

- DK or worsted/Aran weight yarn in grey, parchment and cream

- 4-ply cotton yarn in pink, powder pink, lemon, purple, cherry red, coral, vivid blue and apple green

- Donut making kit list (see **Basic Donut Pattern**)

- Safety eyes, 2 x 10–14mm*, or black yarn or black embroidery thread to make your own

*Safety eyes should **only** be used for children aged three years or older.*

Sew on the large rein before sewing the smaller ones either side of the mouth. This will speed up the assembly.

DONUT

Follow the **Basic Donut Pattern** to create the donut base in grey and the icing in parchment, omitting the sprinkles.

EARS (MAKE 2)

Using 3mm hook and cream, make a magic ring.

Round 1: 6 sc into ring. (6 sts)

Round 2: 1 sc in each st around.

Round 3: [2 sc, 2 sc in next st] twice. (8 sts)

Round 4: 1 sc in each st around.

Round 5: [1 sc, 2 sc in next st] 4 times. (12 sts)

Rounds 6 to 9: 1 sc in each st around.

Round 10: [1 sc, inv dec] 4 times. (8 sts)

Slst in next st, fasten off, cut yarn, leaving a long tail for sewing. Attach ears on each side of the Donut hole at the back of the icing, evenly spaced apart. Sew random sprinkles on the ears using some or all of the lemon, purple, cherry red, coral, vivid blue and apple green yarn.

EYES

If using safety eyes, place them between rounds 4 and 5 of the icing, evenly spaced apart. Alternatively, to make the toy suitable for children under three years of age, you can crochet or embroider the eyes (see **Basic Donut Pattern: Eyes**).

MUZZLE

Using 3mm hook and cream, make a magic ring.

Round 1: 6 sc into ring. (6 sts)

Round 2: 2 sc in each st around. (12 sts)

Round 3: [1 sc, 2 sc in next st] 6 times. (18 sts)

Round 4: [2 sc, 2 sc in next st] 6 times. (24 sts)

Rounds 5 to 7: 1 sc in each st around.

Slst in next st, fasten off, cut yarn, leaving a long tail for sewing. Lightly stuff and attach below the Donut hole, adding a Y-shape in powder pink for the nose.

FRONT REINS

Using 3mm hook and pink, make 5 ch.

Row 1: 1 sc into 2nd ch from hook and in next 3 sts, turn. (4 sts)

Rows 2 to 13: 1 ch, 1 sc in each st, turn.

Fasten off, cut yarn, leaving a long tail for sewing. Attach to top of muzzle.

SIDE REINS (MAKE 2)

Using 3mm hook and pink, make 5 ch.

Row 1: 1 sc into 2nd ch from hook and in next 3 sts, turn. (4 sts)

Rows 2 to 8: 1 ch, 1 sc in each st, turn.

Fasten off, cut yarn leaving a long tail for sewing. Attach to each side of the muzzle as shown.

EAR TASSELS

Using lemon, purple, cherry red, coral, vivid blue and a darning needle, weave through the tips of the ears and securely fasten. Trim the excess with scissors leaving a 1cm long yarn strand sticking up from the tip of the ear.

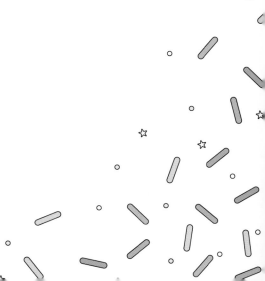

Hamster

This cute-as-a-button Donut Buddy can't wait to come home with you! He loves to nibble on fruit and vegetables, so make sure he has lots of treats!

YOU WILL NEED

- Size 3mm (US C/2 or D/3) and 4mm (US G/6) hooks
- DK or worsted/Aran weight yarn in peach, camel, cream, powder pink and walnut
- 4-ply cotton yarn in pink
- Donut making kit list (see **Basic Donut Pattern**)
- Safety eyes, 2 x 10–14mm*, or black yarn or black embroidery thread to make your own

*Safety eyes should **only** be used for children aged three years or older.*

DONUT

Follow the **Basic Donut Pattern** to create the donut base in peach.

ICING

Leaving a long tail for sewing, carry the unused colour yarn along when you change colours throughout. Work in continuous rounds with no starting ch after round 1.

Using 4mm hook and cream, make 10 ch, change to camel, make 10 ch, change to cream join ch into a circle with a slst. (10 cream, 10 camel sts)

Round 1: Using cream, 1 ch (does not count as a st), [1 sc, 2 sc in next st] 5 times, change to camel, [1 sc, 2 sc in next st] 5 times. (15 cream, 15 camel sts)

Round 2: Change to cream, 15 sc, change to camel, 15 sc.

Round 3: Change to cream, [2 sc, 2 sc in next st] 5 times, change to camel, [2 sc, 2 sc in next st] 5 times. (20 cream, 20 camel sts)

Round 4: Change to cream, 20 sc, change to camel, 20 sc.

Round 5: Change to cream, [3 sc, 2 sc in next st] 5 times, change to camel, [3 sc, 2 sc in next st] 5 times. (25 cream, 25 camel sts)

Attach safety eyes between rounds 4 and 5 of the camel coloured section.

Rounds 6 to 8: Change to cream, 25 sc, change to camel, 25 sc.

Round 9: Change to cream, (drip 1) 1 sc, 1 hdc, 1 dc, 1 trc, 1 dc, 1 hdc, 3 sc; (drip 2) 1 hdc, 1 dc, 2 trc, 1 dc, 3 sc; (drip 3) 1 hdc, 2 dc, 1 hdc, 3 sc; (drip 4) 1 hdc, change to camel, 1 dc, 2 trc, 1 dc, 1 hdc, 3 sc; (drip 5) 1 hdc, 2 dc, 1 trc, 1 dc, 1 hdc, 3 sc; (drip 6) 2 hdc, 3 dc, 3 sc. (50 sts)

Slst in next st, fasten off, cut yarn, leaving a long tail for sewing together.

SPRINKLES

Using a small amount of walnut and a darning needle, weave in small sprinkle lines on the lower part of the body from the back to the front of the icing, take yarn to the back and fasten off.

Sew the icing onto the Donut starting from the small hole in the centre, then sew the edges of the icing to secure.

EYES

If using safety eyes, place them between rounds 4 and 5 of the icing, evenly spaced apart. Alternatively, to make the toy suitable for children under three years of age, you can crochet or embroider the eyes (see **Basic Donut Pattern: Eyes**).

EARS (MAKE 2)

Using 3mm hook and peach, make a magic ring.

Round 1: 6 sc into ring. (6 sts)

Change to camel.

Round 2: 2 sc in each st around. (12 sts)

Round 3: [1 sc, 2 sc in next st] 6 times. (18 sts)

Slst in next st, fasten off, cut yarn, leaving a long tail for sewing. Attach the ears to the back of the Donut, evenly spaced apart.

ARMS (MAKE 2)

Using 3mm hook and powder pink, make a magic ring.

Round 1: 6 sc into ring. (6 sts)

Round 2: 1 sc in each st around.

Change to camel.

Round 3: [1 sc, 2 sc in next st] 3 times. (9 sts)

Rounds 4 to 9: 1 sc in each st around.

Slst in next st, fasten off, cut yarn leaving a long tail for sewing. Attach the arms on either side of body.

LEG TOP (MAKE 2)

Using 3mm hook and camel, make a magic ring.

Round 1: 6 sc into ring. (6 sts)

Round 2: 2 sc in each st around. (12 sts)

Round 3: [1 sc, 2 sc in next st] 6 times. (18 sts)

Rounds 4 to 5: 1 sc in each st around.

Slst in next st, fasten off, cut yarn, leaving a long tail for sewing. Stuff and attach a leg top on either side of the Donut.

FEET (MAKE 2)

Using 3mm hook and camel, make a magic ring.

Round 1: 6 sc into ring. (6 sts)

Round 2: 2 sc in each st around. (12 sts)

Rounds 3 to 5: 1 sc in each st around.

Slst in next st, fasten off, cut yarn, leaving a long tail for sewing. Stuff and attach a foot on either side of the Donut, overlapping the leg top.

CHEEKS (MAKE 2)

Using 3mm hook and cream, make a magic ring.

Round 1: 6 sc into ring. (6 sts)

Round 2: 2 sc in each st around. (12 sts)

Rounds 3 to 4: 1 sc in each st around.

Slst in next st, fasten off, cut yarn, leaving a long tail for sewing. Lightly stuff and attach the cheeks just below the eyes, evenly spaced apart.

NOSE

Using a darning needle and pink thread, sew a small horizontal nose between the eyes 3 sts wide.

Penguin

This dapper chap is usually found waddling around on ice, but today he's ready to play! He loves hanging out with his donut friends and exchanging bow ties with the other penguins!

YOU WILL NEED

- Size 3mm (US C/2 or D/3) and 4mm (US G/6) hooks
- DK or worsted/Aran weight yarn in black, white, citron and red
- Donut making kit list (see **Basic Donut Pattern**)
- Safety eyes, 2 x 10–14mm*, or black yarn or black embroidery thread to make your own

*Safety eyes should **only** be used for children aged three years or older.*

DONUT

Follow the **Basic Donut Pattern** to create the donut base in black.

ICING

Leaving a long tail for sewing, work in continuous rounds with no starting ch after round 1.

Using 4mm hook and white, make 20 ch, join ch into a circle with a slst.

Round 1: 1 ch (does not count as a st), [1 sc, 2 sc in next st] 10 times. (30 sts)

Round 2: 1 sc in each st around.

Round 3: [2 sc, 2 sc in next st] 10 times. (40 sts)

Round 4: 1 sc in each st around.

Round 5: [3 sc, 2 sc in next st] 10 times. (50 sts)

Attach safety eyes between rounds 4 and 5.

Change to black.

Rounds 6 to 8: 1 sc in each st around.

Round 9: (Drip 1) 1 sc, 1 hdc, 1 dc, 1 trc, 1 dc, 1 hdc, 3 sc; (drip 2) 1 hdc, 1 dc, 2 trc, 1 dc, 3 sc; (drip 3) 1 hdc, 2 dc, 1 hdc, 3 sc; (drip 4) 1 hdc, 1 dc, 2 trc, 1 dc, 1 hdc, 3 sc; (drip 5) 1 hdc, 2 dc, 1 trc, 1 dc, 1 hdc, 3 sc; (drip 6) 2 hdc, 3 dc, 3 sc. (50 sts)

Slst in next st, fasten off, cut yarn, leaving a long tail for sewing together. Sew the icing onto the Donut starting from the small hole in the centre, then sew the edges of the icing to secure.

WHITE ICING TRIM

Ch as many sts as you will need to fit around the outer white of the icing. Fasten off, cut yarn leaving a long tail for sewing. Sew the trim around the outer edge of the white part of the icing.

BEAK

Using 3mm hook and citron, make a magic ring.

Round 1: 6 sc into ring. (6 sts)

Round 2: 2 sc in each st around. (12 sts)

Rounds 3 to 4: 1 sc in each st around.

Slst in next st, fasten off, cut yarn leaving a long tail for sewing. Fold in half and attach to the Donut.

EYES (MAKE 2)

Using 3mm hook and white, make a magic ring.

Round 1: 6 sc into ring. (6 sts)

Round 2: 2 sc in each st around. (12 sts)

Slst in next st, fasten off, cut yarn, leaving a long tail for sewing. Securely place safety eyes in the centre of the white circles if using them. Alternatively, to make the toy suitable for children under three years of age, you can crochet or embroider the eyes (see **Basic Donut Pattern: Eyes**). Attach the eyes to the Donut on either side of the beak.

WINGS (MAKE 2)

Using 3mm hook and black, make a magic ring.

Round 1: 6 sc into ring. (6 sts)

Round 2: 2 sc in each st around. (12 sts)

Round 3: [1 sc, 2 sc in next st] 6 times. (18 sts)

Rounds 4 to 7: 1 sc in each st around.

Round 8: [7 sc, inv dec] twice. (16 sts)

Round 9: [6 sc, inv dec] twice. (14 sts)

Round 10: [5 sc, inv dec] twice. (12 sts)

Round 11: 1 sc in each st around.

Round 12: [4 sc, inv dec] twice. (10 sts)

Round 13: 1 sc in each st around.

Round 14: [3 sc, inv dec] twice. (8 sts)

Round 15: 1 sc in each st around.

Round 16: [2 sc, inv dec] twice. (6 sts)

Round 17: [inv dec] 3 times. (3 sts)

Fasten off, cut yarn and weave in ends. Attach each wing on either side of the Donut.

FEET (MAKE 2)

Using 3mm hook and citron, make a magic ring.

Round 1: 6 sc into ring. (6 sts)

Round 2: 2 sc in each st around. (12 sts)

Round 3: [1 sc, 2 sc in next st] 6 times. (18 sts)

Slst in next st, fasten off, cut yarn, leaving a long tail for sewing. Attach each foot, evenly spaced apart, at the bottom of the Donut.

FINISHING TOUCHES

To add a bow to your penguin, make one in red (see **Accessories**), then sew securely under the beak.

Highland Cow

This handsome cow has just had a haircut! He loves to play with other animals, and has a long woolly coat to keep him warm in the chilly Scottish Highlands.

YOU WILL NEED

- Size 2.5mm (US B/1), 3mm (US C/2 or D/3) and 4mm (US G/6) hooks

- DK or worsted/Aran weight yarn in beige, stone, cream and caramel

- 4-ply cotton yarn in yellow

- Donut making kit list (see **Basic Donut Pattern**)

- Safety eyes, 2 x 10–14mm*, or black yarn or black embroidery thread to make your own

*Safety eyes should **only** be used for children aged three years or older.

Add lots of different coloured strands of yarn to the hair for a fun look. Make sure to tightly fasten them off as you work each strand through.

DONUT

Follow the **Basic Donut Pattern** to create the donut base in beige and the icing in stone, omitting the sprinkles.

EYES

If using safety eyes, place them between rounds 4 and 5 of the icing, evenly spaced apart. Alternatively, to make the toy suitable for children under three years of age, you can crochet or embroider the eyes (see **Basic Donut Pattern: Eyes**).

EARS (MAKE 2)

Using 3mm hook and stone, make a magic ring.

Round 1: 6 sc into ring. (6 sts)

Round 2: [1 sc, 2 sc in next st] 3 times. (9 sts)

Round 3: 1 sc in each st around.

Round 4: [2 sc, 2 sc in next st] 3 times. (12 sts)

Round 5: [3 sc, 2 sc in next st] 3 times. (15 sts)

Rounds 6 to 8: 1 sc in each st around.

Slst in next st, fasten off, cut yarn, leaving a long tail for sewing. Attach the ears, evenly spaced apart.

HORNS (MAKE 2)

Using 2.5mm hook and cream, make a magic ring.

Round 1: 6 sc into ring. (6 sts)

Round 2: 2 sc in the first st, 5 sc. (7 sts)

Round 3: 2 sc in the first st, 6 sc. (8 sts)

Round 4: 2 sc in the first st, 7 sc. (9 sts)

Round 5: 2 sc in the first st, 8 sc. (10 sts)

Round 6: 2 sc in the first st, 9 sc. (11 sts)

Slst in next st, fasten off, cut yarn, leaving a long tail for sewing. Lightly stuff and attach, evenly spaced apart.

MUZZLE

Using 3mm hook and cream, make 10 ch.

Round 1: starting in the 2nd ch from hook, 8 sc, 3 sc in next st, continue on other side of foundation ch, 7 sc, 2 sc in next st. (20 sts)

Round 2: 2 sc in first st, 7 sc, 2 sc in next 3 sts, 7 sc, 2 sc in next 2 sts. (26 sts)

Rounds 3 to 4: 1 sc in each st around.

Slst in next st, fasten off, cut yarn, leaving a long tail for sewing.

NOSE RING

Using 2.5mm hook and yellow, leaving a long tail at both ends for sewing, make 8 ch.

Fasten off, cut yarn, leaving a long tail. (8 sts)

NOSTRILS (MAKE 2)

Using 2.5mm hook and caramel, make a magic ring.

Round 1: 5 sc into ring. (5 sts)

Slst in next st, fasten off, cut yarn, leaving a long tail for sewing. Lightly stuff and attach the muzzle, adding the nostrils and nose ring.

HAIR

(See **Crochet Techniques: Attaching the Hair** to see the basic technique for attaching the hair.)

Using two different colours of yarn, cut 10 strands of each. Securely sew each strand between the ears at the top of the icing, adding a different colour strand to each section. Cut to 5cm, so it sits nicely on top of the eyes and lightly brush to give a fluffy effect.

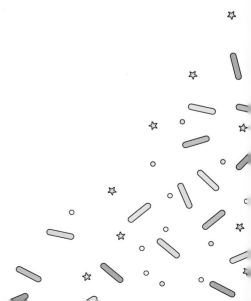

Toucan

This bright and bubbly bird is a sight to be seen and loves to play outdoors! Her long colourful beak helps her to stand out amongst the crowd in the rainforests.

YOU WILL NEED

- 3mm (US C/2 or D/3) and 4mm (US G/6) hooks
- DK or worsted/Aran weight yarn in yellow, black, green, turquoise, pink, red, blue and white
- Embroidery thread in yellow and green
- Donut making kit list (see **Basic Donut Pattern**)
- Safety eyes, 2 x 10–14mm*, or black yarn or black embroidery thread to make your own

*Safety eyes should **only** be used for children aged three years or older.*

DONUT

Follow the Basic Donut Pattern to create the donut base in yellow and the icing in black, omitting the sprinkles.

BEAK

Using 3mm hook and red, make a magic ring.

Round 1: 6 sc into ring. (6 sts)

Round 2: 2 sc in each st around. (12 sts)

Round 3: [1 sc, 2 sc in next st] 6 times. (18 sts)

Round 4: [2 sc, 2 sc in next st] 6 times. (24 sts)

Change to pink.

Round 5: [3 sc, 2 sc in next st] 6 times. (30 sts)

Round 6: [inv dec, 1 sc] 3 times, [2 sc in next st, 6 sc] 3 times. (30 sts)

Round 7: [inv dec] 3 times, [2 sc in next st, 7 sc] 3 times. (30 sts)

Round 8: 1 sc in each st around.

Change to blue.

Rounds 9 to 12: 1 sc in each st around.

Change to green.

Rounds 13 to 16: 1 sc in each st around.

Change to yellow.

Rounds 17 to 19: 1 sc in each st around.

Round 20: [3 sc, inv dec] 6 times. (24 sts)

Slst in next st, fasten off, cut yarn, leaving a long tail for sewing. Stuff firmly, then attach to one side of Donut.

EYES (MAKE 2)

Using 3mm hook and white, make a magic ring.

Round 1: 6 sc into ring. (6 sts)

Round 2: 2 sc in each st around. (12 sts)

Round 3: [1 sc, 2 sc in next st] 6 times. (18 sts)

Slst in next st, fasten off, cut yarn, leaving a long tail for sewing. If using safety eyes, attach them to the centre of the white patch, adding yellow and green embroidery stitches around each half of the eye. Alternatively, to make the toy suitable for children under three years of age, you can crochet or embroider the eyes (see **Basic Donut Pattern: Eyes**). Attach the eyes to the Donut.

WINGS (MAKE 2)

Using 3mm hook and black, make a magic ring, leaving a long tail for sewing.

Round 1: 6 sc into ring. (6 sts)

Round 2: 2 sc in each st around. (12 sts)

Round 3: [1 sc, 2 sc in next st] 6 times. (18 sts)

Change to red.

Round 4: 1 sc in each st around.
Change to green.

Round 5: 1 sc in each st around.
Change to yellow.

Round 6: 1 sc in each st around.
Change to black.

Round 7: 1 sc in each st around.

Round 8: [7 sc, inv dec] twice. (16 sts)

Round 9: [6 sc, inv dec] twice. (14 sts)

Round 10: [5 sc, inv dec] twice. (12 sts)

Round 11: 1 sc in each st around.

Round 12: [4 sc, inv dec] twice. (10 sts)

Round 13: 1 sc in each st around.

Round 14: [3 sc, inv dec] twice. (8 sts)

Round 15: 1 sc in each st around.

Round 16: [2 sc, inv dec] twice. (6 sts)

Round 17: [inv dec] 3 times. (3 sts)

Fasten off, cut yarn and weave in ends. Attach each wing just below Donut hole.

CHEST PATCH

Using 3mm hook and white, make a magic ring.

Round 1: 6 sc into a magic ring (6 sts)

Round 2: 2 sc into each st all the way around (12 sts)

Round 3: 1 sc into the first st, 2 sc into the next st; repeat all the way around. (18 sts)

Round 4: 2 sc into the next 3 sts, 1 sc into the next 6 sts, 2 sc into the next 3 sts, 1 sc into the next 6 sts, slst into the next st, fasten off, cut yarn, leaving a long tail for sewing. (24 sts)

Using a darning needle, sew on the chest patch just under the toucan's beak securely. Fasten off and weave in ends.

FOOT

Using 3mm hook and blue, make 7 ch.

Round 1: 1 sc in 2nd ch from the hook and in next 4 sts, 2 sc in next st, working in opposite side of foundation ch, 5 sc, 2 sc in next st. (14 sts)

Rounds 2 to 4: 1 sc in each st around.

Round 5: [5 sc, inv dec] twice. (12 sts)

Round 6: [2 sc, inv dec] 3 times. (9 sts)

Rounds 7 to 8: 1 sc in each st around.

Round 9: Working into the blo; 1 sc in each st around.

Rounds 10 to 12: 1 sc in each st around.

Slst in next st, fasten off, cut yarn leaving a long tail for sewing. Attach just below the chest patch.

TAIL

Using 3mm hook and black, make a magic ring.

Round 1: 6 sc into a magic ring

Round 2: 2 sc in each st around. (12 sts)

Rounds 3 to 7: 1 sc in each st around.

Round 8: [2 sc, inv dec] 3 times. (9 sts)

Rounds 9 to 11: 1 sc in each st around.

Slst in next st, fasten off, cut yarn leaving a long tail for sewing. Attach as shown.

Snake

This slithery Donut Buddy is the joker amongst his friends! They all say he's hisss-terical! Make him up with lots of stripes to help him camouflage himself in the long grass.

YOU WILL NEED

- Size 2.5mm (US B/1), 3mm (US C/2 or D/3) and 4mm (US G/6) hooks

- DK or worsted/Aran weight yarn in dark green, light green and citron

- 4-ply cotton yarn in pink

- Donut making kit list (see **Basic Donut Pattern**)

- Safety eyes, 2 x 10–14mm*, or black yarn or black embroidery thread to make your own

*Safety eyes should **only** be used for children aged three years or older.*

DONUT

Follow the Basic Donut Pattern to create the donut base in dark green and the icing in light green, omitting the sprinkles.

HEAD

Using 4mm hook and light green, make a magic ring.

Round 1: 6 sc into ring. (6 sts)

Round 2: [1 sc, 2 sc in next st] 3 times. (9 sts)

Round 3: [2 sc, 2 sc in next st] 3 times. (12 sts)

Round 4: 1 sc in each st around.

Round 5: [3 sc, 2 sc in next st] 3 times. (15 sts)

Round 6: 1 sc in each st around.

Round 7: [4 sc, 2 sc in next st] 3 times. (18 sts)

Round 8: 1 sc in each st around.

Place safety eyes between rounds 7 and 8, 4 sts apart.

Round 9: [2 sc, 2 sc in next st] 6 times. (24 sts)

Rounds 10 to 13: 1 sc in each st around.

Round 14: [2 sc, inv dec] 6 times. (18 sts)

Round 15: [1 sc, inv dec] 6 times. (12 sts)

Round 16: 1 sc in each st around.

Rounds 17 to 18: 6 hdc, 6 sc.

Change to dark green.

Rounds 19 to 20: 6 hdc, 6 sc.

Change to light green.

Round 21: 1 sc in each st around.

Slst in next st, fasten off, cut yarn, leaving a long tail for sewing. Stuff and attach to body central to Donut ring hole.

EYES

If using safety eyes, these will already have been placed when making the head. Alternatively, to make the toy suitable for children under three years of age, you can crochet or embroider the eyes (see **Basic Donut Pattern: Eyes**).

TONGUE

Using 2.5mm hook and pink, make 6 ch.

Row 1: Slst in 2nd ch from hook and in next 2 sts, 3 ch, slst in 2nd ch from the hook and in next st, slst into the next 2 sts.

Fasten off, cut yarn, leaving a long tail for sewing. Attach and secure ends inside head.

TAIL

Using 3mm hook and citron, make a magic ring.

Round 1: 4 sc into ring. (4 sts)

Round 2: 2 sc in first st, 3 sc. (5 sts)

Round 3: 2 sc in first st, 4 sc. (6 sts)

Round 4: [2 sc, 2 sc in next st] twice. (8 sts)

Change to light green.

Round 5: Working in blo, 1 sc in each st around.

Round 6: 1 sc in each st around.

Round 7: [3 sc, 2 sc in next st] twice. (10 sts)

Change to dark green.

Round 8: 1 sc in each st around.

Round 9: [4 sc, 2 sc in next st] twice. (12 sts)

Change to light green.

Round 10: 1 sc in each st around.

Round 11: [5 sc, 2 sc in next st] twice. (14 sts)

Change to dark green.

Round 12: 1 sc in each st around.

Round 13: 7 sc, 7 hdc.

Change to light green.

Rounds 14 to 15: 7 sc, 7 hdc.

Change to dark green.

Rounds 16 to 17: 7 sc, 7 hdc.

Change to light green.

Round 18: 1 sc in each st around.

Slst in next st, fasten off, cut yarn, leaving a long tail for sewing and stuff. Attach to opposite end of body from head.

LARGE TRIANGLES (MAKE 6)

Using 3mm hook and dark green, make 6 ch.

Row 1: 1 sc in 2nd ch from the hook and each st across, turn. (5 sts)

Row 2: 1 ch, (does not count as st throughout), 1 sc, inv dec, 2 sc, turn. (4 sts)

Row 3: 1 ch, 1 sc, inv dec, 1 sc, turn. (3 sts)

Row 4: 1 ch, 1 sc, inv dec, turn. (2 sts)

Row 5: 1 ch, inv dec. (1 st)

Fasten off, cut yarn, leaving a long tail for sewing. Attach to icing spaced evenly apart.

CROCHET LINES (MAKE 12)

Using 2.5mm hook and citron, make 9 ch.

Fasten off, cut yarn, leaving a long tail for sewing. (9 sts). Attach lines down 2 sides of each triangle.

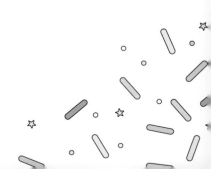

Accessories

With just a little leftover yarn, you can make a range of accessories to add personality to your Donut Buddies.

SMALL FLOWER

Shown on the Bunny, Turtle, Sheep, Snail and Cow.

Using 2.5mm hook, make a magic ring.

Round 1: 5 sc into ring, pull ring tight, slst into first sc. (5 sts)

Round 2: 1 ch (does not count as st), (1 hdc, 3dc, 1hdc) in first st to make petal, [(1 hdc, 3dc, 1hdc) in next st] 4 times, slst in top of 1 ch at the beginning of round and fasten off leaving a long tail to attach to Donut Body. (5 petals)

LARGE FLOWER

Shown on the Elephant.

Using 2.5mm hook and blue, make 36 ch.

Row 1: 1 dc in 6th ch from hook, [miss 2 sts, (1 dc, 2 ch, 1 dc) in next st] 10 times, turn [A]. (11 V sts)

Row 2: 3 ch (counts as st), 1 dc in centre sp of V st, 3 ch, 2 dc in same V st sp [B], [(2 dc, 3 ch, 2 dc) in next V st sp] 10 times, turn [C].

Row 3: 1 ch (does not count as st), [7 dc in V st sp, 1 sc between this and next V st [D]] 10 times, 7 dc in V st sp, 1 sc in last st.

Fasten off, cut yarn, leaving a long tail for sewing [E]. Twist the flower into a spiral shape and sew together to secure [F].

BOW

Shown on the Pig, Hippo and Penguin.

Using 2.5mm hook, make 4 ch.

Row 1: 1 sc in 2nd ch from hook and in each ch along, turn. (3 sts)

Rows 2 to 12: 1 ch (does not count as st), 1 sc in each st, turn. [G]

Fasten off, cut yarn, leaving a long tail for sewing. Sew the bow together by bringing both ends into the centre and sewing each side closed [H]. Wrap the remaining yarn around centre of fold to create a bow shape [I], then attach to your Donut Buddy.

STARFISH

Shown on the Crab and Jellyfish.

Using 2.5mm hook and turquoise for crab or melon pink for jellyfish, make a magic ring. [J]

Round 1: 10 sc into ring. (10 sts)

Round 2: [1 sc, 2 sc in next st] 5 times, slst in top of the first sc. [K] (15 sts)

Round 3: [ch 7, slst in the 2nd ch from hook, 2 sc, 1 hdc, 2 dc, miss next st in magic ring, slst in the next 2 sts] 5 times [L-O]. (5 points)

Fasten off and cut yarn, leaving a long tail for sewing [P].

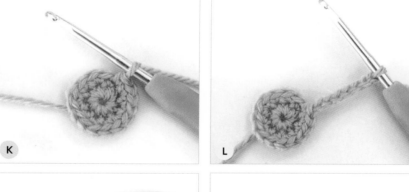

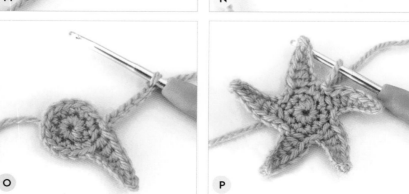

Making Collections

Remember back to when you were young. What was your favourite thing to collect? Help your child learn ways of grouping Donut Buddies together to make their very own collections!

SAFARI ANIMALS

How many animals can you find roaming the plains of Africa or sitting in a tropical swamp? Place them together to make your own Safari collection.

SPRINGTIME

That lovely time of year when flowers are blooming, the sun is shining and Easter is on the horizon. How about making a springtime collection?

FUN DAYS & HOLIDAYS!

You could have a holiday collection – think of all the holidays and fun days there are based on your Donut Buddies – Christmas, Thanksgiving, Halloween, and more. Add in whichever of your buddies fit into this category.

FARM ANIMALS

There are lots of these in your collection! Cows, ducks, sheep, dogs and pigs. What else can you find down on the farm?

UNDER THE SEA

Who's for a paddle about looking for these underwater creatures? How many can you find? Don't forget to look under all the rocks.

DINOSAURS & MADE UP COLLECTIONS

Very old or not real – how many can you place in this group? Your Triceratops might love hanging out with your Unicorn or even an Alien!

Playing Donut Games

These gorgeous Donut Buddies can be used in all sorts of games, from hide and seek to making tea, and from happy families to tiger hunts. Why not try these ideas?

SECRET SAFARI

Become a ranger and head off around the world on a secret safari in your home or garden. "Shhh", be careful not to scare the animals as you explore all of their different habitats. Secret Safari is great for learning about the animal characters and where they live in the world. Have fun exploring!

BAKING & TEA PARTY

Enjoy 'baking' your donuts, then pretend to decorate them with colourful icing and yummy toppings! Serve them at your tea party to all your friends. Don't put them in your mouth though - remember this is just pretend.

SECRET SANTA

For a fun holiday game, why not hide different holiday-themed Donut Buddies around the house, using the hot and cool method for when your children are getting close to finding their prizes.

SPOOKY SURPRISE

Why not do the same at Halloween and have a surprise for whoever finds the spooky Donut Buddy!

STORY TELLING

Make bedtime fun by placing your favourite Donut Buddies into a bag and taking turns pulling them out - now make up a story about that character and let your imagination fly.

ANIMAL FAMILIES

Make large, medium and small Donut Buddies to create animal families. Mix and match accessories to create your perfect set!

LEARNING TO COUNT

Make different Donut Buddy characters and group them into odd or even sets. Add Donut Buddies to the groups or take some away, making learning to count a fun pastime!

Crochet Techniques

Stitches

Slip Knot

When you begin your crochet, you will start with a slip knot. Make a circle with your fingers or hook [1] and pull the yarn through to make a stitch [2].

Chain (ch)

Wrap the yarn over the hook from back to front, known as a yo [1], pull the hook carrying the yarn through the loop already on your hook. You have now completed one chain stitch [2]. Repeat these steps as indicated in the pattern to create a foundation chain.

Back Loop Only (BLO)

Almost every Crochet stitch has a V shape at the top. That V shape is made up of two loops, a front and a back loop. When a pattern says to work in back loop only (BLO), work into the back loop furthest away from you.

These stitches all use US terminology. See **Basic Donut Pattern: Pattern Abbreviations** for the equivalent UK crochet terms.

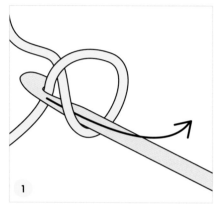

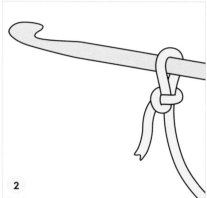

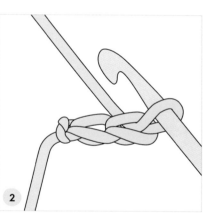

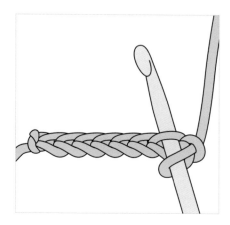

Slip Stitch (slst)

The Slip Stitch is the shortest of all crochet stitches and is more of a technique than an actual stitch. Slip stitches are used to move yarn across a group of stitches without adding height or to join rounds together. Insert the hook into the stitch and yo. Draw the hook through the stitch and loop on your hook at the same time. You have now completed one slip stitch.

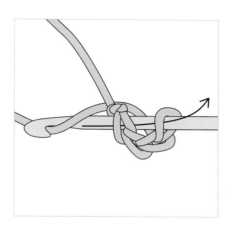

Single Crochet (sc)

Single crochet is the main stitch used in my book. Insert your hook into the next stitch [1], yo, pull the yarn through the stitch [2]. You will now see two loops on the hook, yo again [3] and draw through both loops at once [4]. You have now completed one single crochet stitch. Continue in the same way until you reach the end of the row [5].

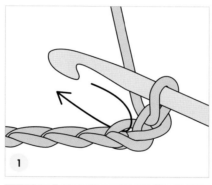

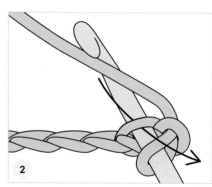

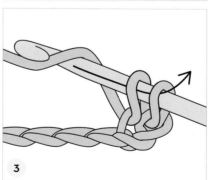

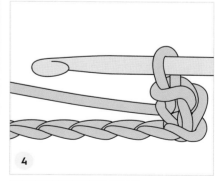

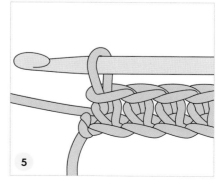

Half Double Crochet (hdc)

The half double crochet falls in-between a single crochet and a double crochet in height, but instead of working through two loops at a time, you draw the yarn through three loops on the hook. Yo, before placing the hook into the stitch [1], yo again and draw through the stitch. You now have three loops on the hook, yo again and pull through all three loops on your hook [2]. You have now completed your first half double crochet stitch. Continue in the same way to the end of the row [3].

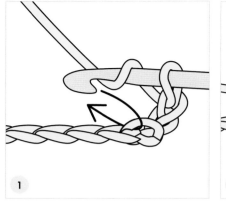

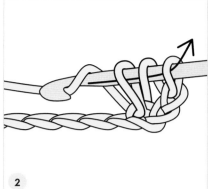

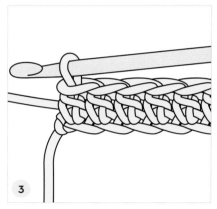

Double Crochet (dc)

Double crochet is a taller stitch than single and half double crochet. Yo, before placing the hook in the stitch [1], yo and draw through the stitch. You now have three loops on the hook [2], yo again and pull through the first two loops, you now have two loops on the hook, yo one last time and bring it through both loops on the hook [3]. You have now completed one Double Crochet stitch. Continue in the same way to the end of the row [4].

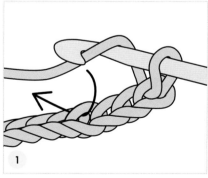

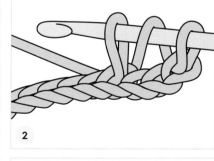

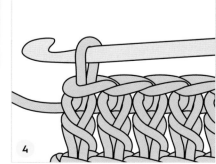

Triple/Treble Crochet (trc)

A triple crochet or treble crochet is taller than a double crochet and is made by working two yarn overs at the start of the stitch. Yo twice [1] and draw yarn through the stitch, *yo again and pull through the first two loops on the hook [2]. Repeat from * twice. You have now completed one Triple Crochet stitch.

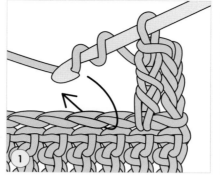
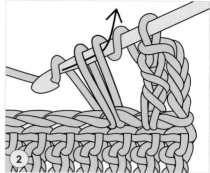

Increasing

To increase, work two single crochet stitches into the same stitch. You have now completed one Increase stitch.

Invisible Decrease (Inv Dec)

The Invisible Decrease method works best for Amigurumi as it creates a much neater finish, and the stitch will look more like the other stitches in the row. Insert your hook into the front loop of your first stitch, insert your hook into the front loop of the next stitch [1], you now have three loops on the hook. Yo and draw through the first two loops on your hook [2], yo again and draw through the remaining two loops on your hook [3]. You have now completed one invisible decrease.

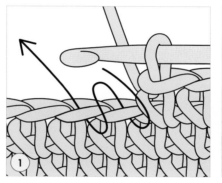
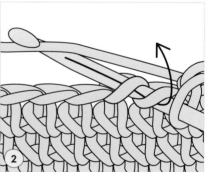
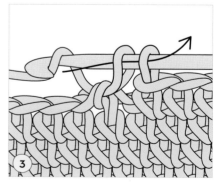

Half Double Crochet Decrease (Hdc Inv Dec)

Yo, before placing your hook into the stitch [1]. Insert your hook through the front loop of the next stitch [2], then insert your hook through the front loop of the following stitch without yarning over again. You should have four loops on your hook [3]. Yo [4], pull through the first two loops; you will now have three loops on the hook [5]. Yo, pull through the remaining three loops on the hook [6]. You have now completed one Half Double Crochet Invisible Decrease.

Half Double Crochet Three Together Decrease (Hdc3tog)

*Yo, insert hook in next stitch, yo [1] and pull up a loop [2], repeat from * twice more. You will now have seven loops on the hook [3], yo and pull through all seven loops on the hook [4]. You have now completed one Half Double Crochet Three Together.

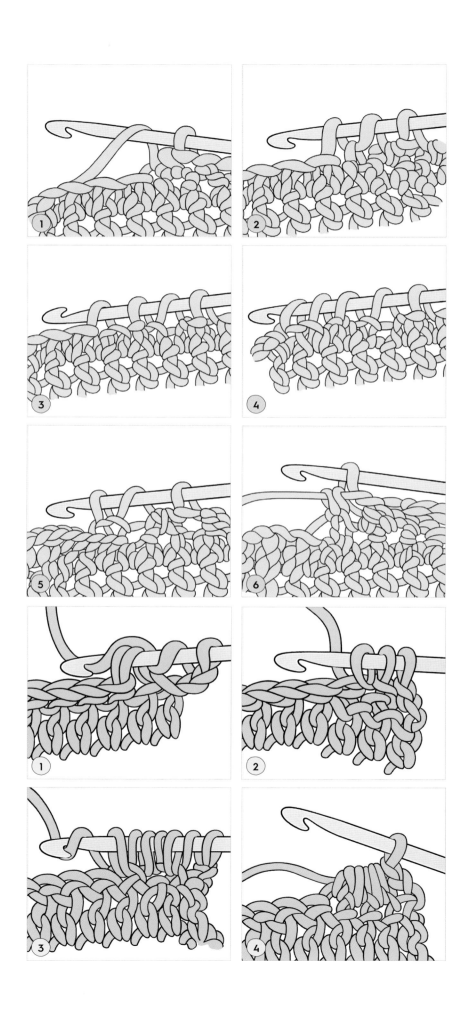

Double Crochet Three Together Decrease (Dc3tog)

*Yo, insert hook in next stitch, yo and pull up loop, yo, draw through 2 loops; repeat from * twice more (4 loops on hook), yo, draw through all loops on hook. You have now completed one Double Crochet three together.

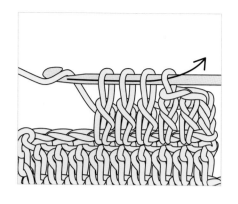

Bobble Stitch

Yo from the back to the front before placing the hook in the stitch. Wrap the yarn over the hook and draw through the stitch. You now have 3 loops on the hook. Wrap the yarn over the hook and pull it through the first two loops. One half closed Double Crochet is complete and 2 loops remain. Repeat 3 more times Into the same stitch, you should have 5 loops on the hook. Wrap the yarn over the hook and through all 5 loops.

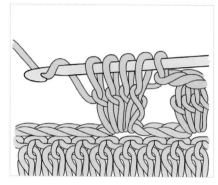

The Bobble Stitch is a cluster of Double Crochet stitches in one stitch which creates a raised 'bump' or bobble in your work.

Shell Stitch

A shell stitch is a combination of a single crochet stitch and a 'shell' that consists of 5 double crochet stitches (less double crochet stitches can be used). The shell and the single crochets alternate. Work 1 sc in the first stitch, then *yo, insert the hook into the third stitch along [1], yo and pull through the stitch, yo and pull through 2 loops on the hook, yo and pull through remaining 2 loops. Repeat from * 4 more times into the same stitch. Single crochet into the third stitch along [2].

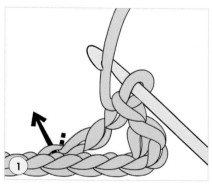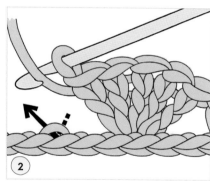

Attaching the Hair

Using your crochet hook or darning needle and your chosen colour yarn; place your hook or needle through the stitch you wish to attach the hair to. If using a darning needle, pull a strand of yarn through until it's halfway point rests under the stitch, then tie a knot tightly in the yarn to secure. If using a crochet hook, pull through the folded end of the yarn loop, then bring the remaining yarn through the loop and pull tight.

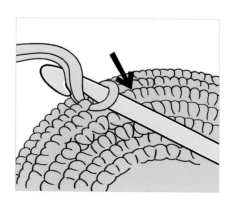

Techniques

Working in the Round

The term 'round' in crochet simply means working around a circle of stitches. You will work in the round for most Amigurumi projects. Sometimes you use a slip stitch to join to the first stitch when working in rounds, and sometimes, you will work in a continuous spiral. When working in a spiral, always use a stitch marker to mark the last stitch of each round and move up as you work. You will increase in a number of places as the work grows to keep a circle shape.

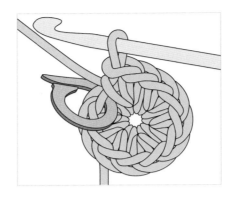

Working Around a Magic Ring

A magic ring is a way to begin crocheting in the round by crocheting the first round into an adjustable loop and then pulling the loop tight. To create a magic ring, wrap the yarn around two fingers and hold the point where the loop overlaps between your index finger and thumb [1]. Insert your hook into the loop, from the front to the back, and pull up a loop, yo and pull through the loop on your hook [2]. Now work the required number of stitches into the loop.

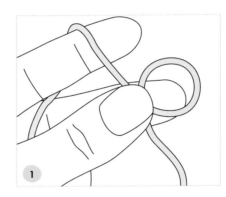
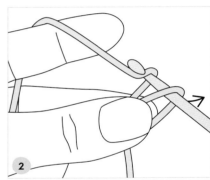

Working Around a Foundation Chain

Some of my facial features start with an oval shape instead of a circle. You make an oval by crocheting around a foundation chain instead of a magic ring. You crochet along the foundation chain [1], turn the piece at the end and then work in the single loops at the underside of the foundation chain [2]. In order to maintain a smooth oval shape, you increase in the stitches at the rounded sides of the oval [3].

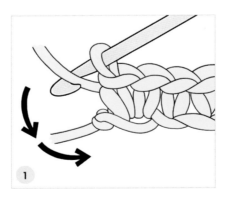
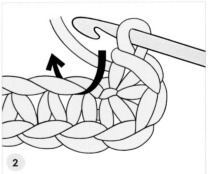
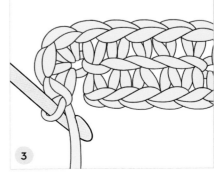

Colour Changes

When you want to change colours neatly, you will need to work your last stitch with one colour before yarning over and through with the new colour. To do this, make the next stitch as usual, but don't pull the final loop through. Wrap your new colour of yarn over your hook [1] and pull it through the remaining loops [2]. Then carry on making stitches with the new colour [3].

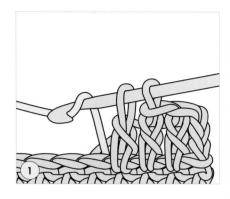
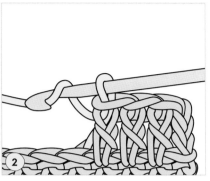
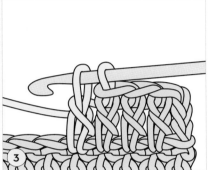

Fastening Off

Fastening off is an important step in crochet as it means that all of the stitches in your crocheted creation will stay put. Fastening off the ends also means that there is less risk of the yarn ends getting caught and undoing all of your careful work.
To fasten off, simply make a single crochet at the end of your work, cut the yarn and pull it tightly, then either weave in your ends securely or leave a long tail for sewing.

Right Side of Work

When sewing your donuts, make sure that you have the right side of the crochet facing outwards. In the examples to the right, you can see the right side versus the wrong side.

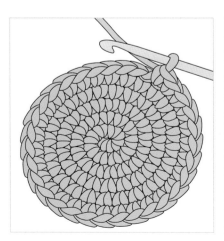

Right side

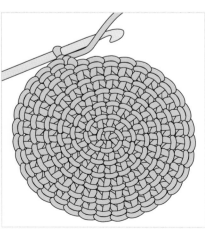

Wrong side

Acknowledgements

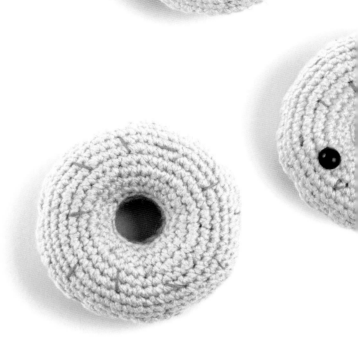

Firstly I would like to thank my family for their constant support throughout my crochet career. To my mother and father, who have helped keep me focused and supported me during this exciting time in my life and to my children, who are the reason I started to crochet; you are my inspiration, and I love you lots!

I would like to take the time to thank David and Charles for this incredible opportunity. It has been one of the most rewarding times of my life, and I'm so happy you enjoy my Donut Buddies as much as I do.

I also want to thank my crochet supporters. You have all been amazing! Thank you for believing in me and enjoying my work. So many of you have made my Donut Buddies around the world, and I have loved seeing them all.

About the Author

Rachel Zain is a crochet designer who loves cute, kawaii crochet designs, especially donuts! She has a passion for crafting and loves handmade toys. When she's not crocheting, she loves to spend time outdoors with her children, travelling and discovering new places; she also likes to collect little trinkets from each place she visits.

Rachel lives in the UK with her parents and two children. You can find her patterns on Etsy and Ravelry. Follow her day-to-day Crochet creations on Instagram @Oodles_of_Crochet or on Facebook @Oodlesofcrochetcrafts

Index

A DAVID AND CHARLES BOOK
© David and Charles, Ltd 2022

David and Charles is an imprint of David and Charles, Ltd
Suite A, Tourism House, Pynes Hill, Exeter, EX2 5WS

Text and Designs © Rachel Zain 2022
Layout and Photography © David and Charles, Ltd 2022

First published in the UK and USA in 2022

ISBN-13: 9781446308882 paperback
ISBN-13: 9781446381021 EPUB
ISBN-13: 9781446381014 PDF

This book has been printed on paper from approved
suppliers and made from pulp from sustainable sources.

Printed in the UK by Page Bros for:
David and Charles, Ltd
Suite A, Tourism House, Pynes Hill, Exeter, EX2 5WS

10 9 8 7 6 5 4 3 2

Publishing Director: Ame Verso
Editor: Jessica Cropper
Project Editors: Carol Ibbetson, Cheryl Brown and
Roisin McKenna
Technical Editor: Carol Ibbetson
Head of Design: Sam Staddon
Designer: Lucy Waldron
Pre-press Designer: Ali Stark
Illustrations: Kuo Kang Chen and Cathy Brear
Photography: Jason Jenkins
Production Manager: Beverley Richardson

David and Charles publishes high-quality books on
a wide range of subjects. For more information visit
www.davidandcharles.com.

Share your makes with us on social media using
#dandcbooks and follow us on Facebook and Instagram
by searching for @dandcbooks.

Layout of the digital edition of this book may vary
depending on reader hardware and display settings.